Unseen

Jacinta Parsons

16pt

Copyright Page from the Original Book

books that leave an impression

Published by Affirm Press in 2020
Published by Affirm Press in 2020
28 Thistlethwaite Street, South Melbourne, VIC 3205
www.affirmpress.com.au

Text and copyright © Jacinta Parsons, 2020
All rights reserved. No part of this publication may be reproduced without prior permission of the publisher.

Title: UNSEEN / Jacinta Parsons, author

 A catalogue record for this book is available from the National Library of Australia

Cover design by Karen Wallis, Taloula Press
Typeset in Bembo 12/18 pt by Affirm Press

TABLE OF CONTENTS

introduction	iii
one: a storm brewing	1
two: on illness	19
three: the search for an answer	34
four: two magic words	64
five: a big bag of pills	81
six: living in grey	97
seven: trust and betrayal	116
eight: the body public	138
nine: unseen	154
ten: the face of death	171
eleven: aboard a sinking ship	194
twelve: return to the world	221
thirteen: the impossible becomes real	244
fourteen: a new life	266
fifteen: a place in the system	290
sixteen: seen	306
acknowledgements	323
references	330

Jacinta Parsons is a broadcaster, radio maker, writer and public speaker. She currently hosts *Afternoons* on ABC Melbourne delivering a popular mix of art, culture and ideas. She began her radio life at community radio station Triple R, where she hosted several shows including *Breakfasters* and *Detour*. But her peak Melbourne moment came earlier, when she worked as a tram conductor (proudly wearing one of the last of the Connie's green uniforms).

Jacinta has lived with Crohn's disease for most of her adult life. She is an ambassador for the Crohn's and Colitis Association, and speaks and writes about the impact of living with chronic illness. She is also an active member of the arts and music community, and is a board member for Rollercoaster, a company of actors with intellectual disabilities. *Unseen* is her first book.

For The Lolo Brothers & Co.
AJ, Mika and Perry. To my eternal loves and the
worlds we have seen together,
in and out of The Nothingness.

***

Bring forth the beauty of your heart
This undying love is who you are
Don't look down
You are not alone
Love will lift you home
Love will make us home
– 'Human', Sol Seppy

introduction

Several years ago, when I first tried to write about chronic illness, I found myself suddenly lost, dredging down into an abyss; it seemed I had inadvertently travelled into a deep darkness, equipped with only a small headlamp.

I'd been asked to speak about the cliffhanger moment in my life at a *Women of Letters* event, and I chose to write about my experience of illness, but as I wrote I found myself confronted with a surprising grief. I sat at the kitchen table and wrote, and cried, and clutched at my stomach. I hadn't known it, but the grief had been waiting there patiently, ready to emerge fully grown as soon as even the smallest amount of attention was paid to it. Its energy surprised me. How close it was to the surface surprised me. It had been incubating for decades, ever since that first moment when I noticed blood pooling at the bottom of the toilet. I had to go over the letter again and again until I was able to get through it without crying.

Since even before I was finally diagnosed with Crohn's disease, my days had been full with illness: the drugs, the pain, the explanations, the working out how to keep going. To avoid choking on the enormity of dealing with the grief over my illness, I had broken it down into tiny pieces. As the saying goes, 'there is only one way to eat an elephant: a bite at a time'. But by separating those pieces from the whole, I had lost sight of the truth. This story had to be understood as *one* thing, to be strung together with a single thread.

When you're in the middle of dealing with a chronic illness, it is usually a series of days that run into weeks that run into months that soon you're counting in years. It's difficult to pull yourself out. When I did finally confront the story of my illness as a whole, sitting at the kitchen table that day, all I could see was how much I had lost. It undid me; I realised how profoundly I had been changed. The person I'd been before I got sick, and the person who I might have become, were both gone. And that feeling of loss, that grief that sat just beneath the surface, needed to find its way out of me.

I had never imagined that I would write this book. Among many other reasons, I didn't feel like I had much of a story to tell: when I was in my early twenties, I was diagnosed with a chronic disease, Crohn's disease. It's just a sentence really, but it's also responsible for everything I currently am. In this book, I hope to somehow capture invisible chronic illness, even if my experience is just a small part of a much larger, amorphous thing.

According to the Australian Institute of Health and Welfare, approximately 50 per cent of the Australian population reports having a chronic illness. The term 'chronic illness' encompasses illnesses as varied as asthma and cancer, Alzheimer's disease and diabetes, chronic fatigue syndrome, HIV/AIDS and a broad range of mental health conditions. Sometimes they have visible symptoms; often they don't. Sometimes they can be debilitating or even fatal; sometimes they can be managed with little disruption to daily existence. The only thing they really have in common is that they cannot be cured. They are illnesses for life.

Of course, when we are talking about an experience that many people go through, there are no absolutes, but I've longed to explain my experience of chronic illness in all its kaleidoscopic glory ever since the day I was diagnosed. When a chronic illness is invisible, as mine is, it can affect your life in unique and complex ways. I wanted to stitch together the mundane story of day-to-day sickness with the reality that illness was also grand and full of terror and wonder, and harboured some of the greatest and worst moments of my life.

I also saw that same longing in other people – the desire to explain that this experience transcended the 'normal' experience of illness. I have spoken to virtual strangers about our shared experience of chronic illness and have ended up in the embrace that you can only share with someone who knows how it feels to live inside your skin. As people right across the invisible illness spectrum reflected the experience that I'd had with Crohn's disease, I began to understand that our stories were shared. Finding out that you're not alone can itself be transformative. What was also resounding, and reflected by so many, was just how isolating invisible illness is. When you can't see anyone else like you, it's easy to believe that you might be the only one.

Illness is like a natural disaster. In that way, it is simple, because you have little choice but to accept it. The only choice left to you is how to respond, and disaster becomes an opportunity. It demands that you move into the present and deal with it immediately. It forces you to look directly into it and into yourself, and to begin to know yourself as it reveals you: bare, naked and true. But the time comes when you must reckon with the damage. There is a moment when the eye of the storm has passed and you creep out, blinking in the light, to assess just exactly what it has done.

Though this book is primarily the story of my own illness, it also travels through the lives of many people who have shared their experiences with me. It is by travelling through all these memories and conversations, armed with my headlamp, that I have tried to tell the story of invisible chronic illness in all its colourful complexity. It also leans on the smart people who have spent careers thinking about what this means for us all. It's also vital to note that I come to this experience of illness and hospitals with the privilege of my whiteness. I acknowledge that although I have attempted, I have a vastly limited ability to truly express or understand the difference of experience and discrimination that First Nations people or people from diverse cultural backgrounds have within our health system.

There is no one story of illness, but there are threads that wind their way around all of us. They reveal that, in many ways, our illnesses are more alike than perhaps we might have known.

***

I had almost finished writing this book when the world stopped, dead in its tracks. It felt like the stories that I had read about the people of Pompeii, who, suddenly and seemingly out of nowhere, had their entire town destroyed by a volcano eruption. Like a diary open to an unfinished final entry, they would be discovered centuries later, fossilised in place, their lives extinguished so fast they barely had time to move.

As so it was when the pandemic hit. Like the great WH Auden poem, 'Funeral Blues', it felt like the world, which had been in a relentless fervour for so long, had finally been put to sleep. The clocks stopped. The streets were emptied. All humanity was forced to face its mortality, and a deep, prolonged and gravely unsettling uncertainty.

The novel coronavirus, or COVID-19, shouldn't have been unexpected, but it was. I remember speaking about it on my radio show, *ABC Afternoons*, when it first began. It was a question on our Friday afternoon quiz – a quirky bit of news that we didn't quite know what to make of: 'Which town in China has been hit by a virus?' The answer was Wuhan, a town not many had heard of until a few weeks before. But it hadn't yet dawned on us what was to come.

In Australia, what tricked us at the start was that serious news events – the really bad things – were always happening to other people over on the other side of the world. Not to us. We have a convenient habit of 'othering' these sorts of experiences to protect ourselves. We imagine that these horrible ordeals could only happen very far away. Even though the numbers were starting to sound frightening, we couldn't imagine that they could ever have anything to do with us.

But soon, what had started as a third or fourth-tier news story became a shocking headline with the word 'pandemic'. I remember I was getting ready for work when I first heard that word, and I stopped mid-thought. *Pandemic,* I mused, and kept brushing my hair, because I'd never heard the word used in this way.

But 'pandemic' came to mean everything, a word so powerful that it shut us down. Slowly, the first signs of fear flashed across our cities.

What surprised me most of all was how the fear could be a greater threat than the pandemic itself. That we could be so alert to our danger that we became a danger to ourselves. At the time, I was catapulted into the same spectrum of fear and uncertainty as nearly everyone around me. If we no longer had a grip on the story, how might it end? We grabbed the toilet paper and the tins of tomatoes in a desperate attempt to control the uncertainty that had winded us. Soon it was the reason we could no longer touch our elderly parents, why our schools closed, why we had to stay inside our homes, why we longed to just bump up against each other on the train.

But as we hunkered down in isolation, what became apparent to me was that this virus, and the way we responded to it, replicated the experience of having a chronic illness. For me it was like muscle memory, each stage mirroring the ones I had gone through when I first became unwell. It was deja vu, but this time, the experience was being shared by the world.

People who have chronic illness have faced these challenges before: isolation, fear, panic buying(!), employment instability, mental health challenges, death, life being utterly transformed in the smallest fraction of time. When cities began to shut down, many people with chronic illness noted that their lives stayed much the same.

And just like the COVID-19 response, chronic illness is initially marked by a period where your normal life is suddenly and abruptly changed. You can't do the things that you normally would – even small things like going to the gym – that make you feel like you. But what is surprising is that sometimes when everything is taken away, the real beauty of our world can appear. There is an opportunity to take a breath and slow down.

We were constantly being told that COVID-19 posed a greater risk for people with chronic illness, particularly those, like me, who are immunosuppressed. For many, it was a marked period of heightened anxiety: since many of our illnesses were hidden, so was our increased vulnerability. And while there was a sense that the world finally had some understanding of how it felt to be ill, there continued to be overwhelming challenges. People with disability and chronic illness began to report being left without some of the crucial support that they relied on to survive day to day. Not only was life-saving medication running low due to panic buying, but some support workers were unable to attend their regular appointments, and regular services all but disappeared. And during every report on a death, we were waiting to hear the words 'underlying medical condition'. For those without chronic illness those words were a comfort. For us, they were the opposite.

By the time you are reading this, you will know more about how this virus ultimately impacted the world than I do right now. We all will. The speed with which this is unfolding is one of its remarkable features. But already I have seen that fear, as it churned through our communities when this all began, has already morphed largely into compassion.

This crisis brought to life the chapters in this book in a way I hadn't anticipated. The way the world has experienced COVID-19 mirrors the way chronic illness impacts us at an individual level. And just like an illness, the virus could be responsible for some grand changes in our lives, and a deeper reflection on who we are and who we want to be.

one

a storm brewing

For many people with chronic illness, their story starts long before the day it is diagnosed, and it can sometimes be hard to recall a time when they were healthy. It is a slow erosion. As simple things become just a little more difficult each day, and you slowly, slowly change your habits to maintain what feels like a normal life, it can be just a matter of weeks before something like eating very little can seem quite ordinary.

Our capacity to adjust to our experience is both our greatest strength and our greatest weakness.

***

My illness began at a time when I was surrounded by illness. It was the early nineties at the time of a recession in Australia, and as I worked my way through a media degree, I was living in run-down, broken houses that I shared with an ever-expanding group of friends. We moved around endlessly from one house to another. The houses we could afford were riddled with damp that ran across the chipped paint on the walls. Usually, the only warmth came from a small heater in the lounge room, and so we would huddle around it and drink wine late into the night.

It was a glorious time of true freedom: freedom from the types of responsibilities that come later in life, the types, I guess, that mean you are an adult. This was that precious moment before we were forced to acknowledge that we had to at least try to work within the system, because it became too tiring living on its fringes. It was a beautiful time of friendship. We looked the same. We dressed the same. We wore each other's clothes. And we thought we only needed each other and believed that it would always be that way. We'd play Kate Bush and Leonard Cohen endlessly and go out to see The Meanies and the Cosmic Psychos in dingy pubs and push against each other at the front of the stage like we were kids wrestling on the grass. It was a joyous time of running full-pace at the wall just to make each other laugh.

And it was intense. During a garbage strike in our neighbourhood in the early 1990s, I was living in a tiny terrace in Richmond with a couple of friends. Garbage was bursting out of large green bags. It had been weeks, and the smell in the neighbourhood seemed to have fused with our clothing and was beginning to live on our skin.

One of my good friends had a wild temper and was beginning to twitch; she began mouthing off about the mound of garbage that had been growing in our backyard. She was distracted by it. Obsessed. She became angry with us, as if we had somehow conspired to ensure the garbage would irritate her.

I'm not entirely clear about what precipitated this exactly, but one evening when the rest of us were out, she grabbed the bags of rubbish we'd been stockpiling and threw them across our lounge-room floor. Rubbish that had been growing increasingly rancid over the weeks was now hanging off our light fittings. It had landed on the couch, it was hidden behind the chairs, and soon it was ground into the already-deteriorating carpet.

We found her breathless and wild-eyed, standing in the corner of the lounge room, triumphant, with no hint of remorse. And that image of her, heaving with victory, with banana peels hanging above her head, remains the lasting picture of what those years of living in share houses had been like. Wild, untamed living.

***

When I met AJ, I was living in a tumble-down house on a small street that backed onto Molly Meldrum's Egyptian-style mansion. Our backyard had been covered in cement, but underneath the house the grass was long and damp, and made it look like we were living on top of a dirty swamp. My housemates and I found some feral kittens hidden in that grass and rescued as many as we could. We kept one, who eventually revealed a split personality. When the moon was full, he would turn into a demon and we would need to vacate the main areas of the house as he prowled, hissing and scratching at the air like he was wrestling with an internal darkness. We called him Tiger for most of the month, but on these nights, we would huddle in our bedrooms speaking of George – the evil cat that controlled our home.

The house was on a street lined with old, tightly packed worker's cottages, built at a time when they could not have imagined the types of tenants that would one day live there. It was the street that inspired Frente's 'Accidentally Kelly Street', and though we didn't know the connection at the time, we lived that song's sunny lyrics. We too had slow adventures that might take days to unravel. I would spend hours listening to Van Morrison's *Astral Weeks* while I painted, carved wood and wrote stories.

I remember, with precise detail, the day that I met AJ. I was wearing blue jeans and a white top embroidered with flowers, and I'd borrowed my housemate's brown boots. I'd plaited the sides of my hair and pulled them back. If I had known I was going to meet the man whose role in my life would become as big as the sky, I might have done more, but you don't get much warning about these things.

I had been playing violin for years, and had done what any self-respecting violinist did in the nineties, which was play a couple of lead breaks in local bands – not well, but I'd had enough classical training to get away with bits and pieces here and there. That day, the drummer of the band, I would be playing for, gave me a lift to the venue in his old car. I had heard about AJ around the traps – everyone knew everyone – but we'd never met before.

I remember the trip in that little car that Saturday morning and the burst of freedom I felt driving out of the centre of the city. They say when you meet 'the one', you know. I did, even though at the time AJ was hiding underneath a large mop of hair. Something happened that day – we had found each other.

Nothing was said at the time, but I think it's true to say that I loved him that day in the way I have always loved him. It felt like it was a love that had always existed, and that all we had to do was just stumble across it. For me, it didn't need to be grown: it was fully fledged from that first moment, and has been that way ever since.

That evening, when I got back home to the little house in Richmond, I sat outside in the concrete garden and had a premonition of us holding our first child. Absurd perhaps – I certainly kept it to myself for many years, and I don't experience this type of thing very often. But it was as if I was watching it on a television screen. It added to my calm surety of what had happened that day.

In the beginning, the pure thrill of having found each other propelled AJ and me through our days. We could finally get to making all the plans that you might make when your team has been assembled. Our plans involved Valiants and long trips and caravans and making art together. But that prescience wasn't there to tell me that we should also have been making plans for illness, and that illness would eclipse any other dream we were dreaming.

***

I began to feel regular tugs, groans and aches all over but I thought they were all part of how my body was supposed to feel. I imagined everyone felt like this – how was I to know they didn't? They would pass soon enough, I thought, like a year of bad weather.

I don't know when I started to ache every time I ate, followed by an unbearable pain pounding in my abdomen that could only be relieved once I'd found a toilet. I'm not sure whether the environment I was living in had any impact on my disease flaring up, but it certainly had an impact on how much emotional space I had to recognise and deal with my symptoms. If we ate anything it was usually bad. We had a night we called 'yellow food night', where we would eat only yellow food: hot chips, potato cakes, battered fish.

Soon my body seemed to know when food was near, and before I'd even eaten, it would become heavy and tired with the knowledge of what was coming. I would remove certain foods from my diet one by one, hoping the reaction might be isolated to that food alone, until there was virtually nothing left. Still, the pain progressed, becoming more severe, and my body's reaction time to food shortened until I had immediate and severe abdominal cramping every time I ate. I loved eating, but it hurt too much. I made myself go hungry for long periods and tried to get through the days of terrible pain.

***

One morning, as sunlight fought through some tiny holes in my blinds and splintered the walls, I rolled over in bed and felt my face. It was stinging and sore. My abdomen dragged inside me like it was trying to exit my body. Then a strong, familiar stabbing pain hit me; I had to move quickly. It was even worse than usual. I swung my aching limbs out of bed and hobbled to the bathroom as fast as I could. Inside, the floor was dripping wet from my housemate's morning shower, and I leaned over the toilet, crouching in the wet, and tried to vomit. This only happened sometimes, when the flare ups got really bad. I was as quiet as I could be. I didn't want the rest of the house to know. My body heaved, every muscle straining as if it was trying to get rid of something. But there was nothing left inside me. My body was simply repelled by itself.

Sickness was becoming so normal that I barely noticed it, or considered it noteworthy. I would hide the ache in my bones and ignore the fevers that would spike when I was run down. It wasn't until I saw photos of myself later, eyes sunk into my head above black bags, that I realised how sick I must have been. Daily, I would push through a fatigue that hung heavy on every muscle, which made simple tasks feel like I was lifting a dead body around. It felt as if the air had been knocked out of me. I barely had energy to find the world amusing anymore.

I knew something was not right, but it was difficult to talk about. My housemates and friends were all sick in some way: anorexia, drug dependence, depression, psychosis and schizophrenia. We were all struggling to function, trying to find ourselves. It's strange to think about now, but that kind of sickness felt quite normal at the time. So for me, everyone else had real stuff happening to them, and my problems were small in comparison. Besides, I was getting used to feeling sick.

From appearances, nobody could have known that I was unwell – except, of course, for the moments when the sickness made its way to the surface and, like a storm, was seen as pain flashing across my face. Even looking at myself in the mirror didn't reveal anything, because this change was cellular, buried underneath so many layers of me that it was entirely invisible.

We hear stories of how people 'just knew' something was wrong. Or about wonder dogs that nuzzle a lump on a leg that turns out to be a cancerous growth. But most of us oscillate between believing that our sickness is the beginning of some fatal disease or playing it down as harmless. We make it fit the narrative that works at the time. That morning, though, as I heaved in the bathroom trying to keep my pain quiet, I knew something would have to change.

After years and years of negotiating the rules of the share-house fridge, attending house meetings and managing the daily chaos of living with as many as five other people in their early twenties, it was time for me to move on. I was tired of moving to a new share-house every six months, and I was sure my lifestyle had contributed to the way I was feeling. Since leaving home I'd had forty housemates in ten or so houses, and a long series of adventures that were sometimes funny, sometimes frightening, but mostly always on the edge of chaos. It was time for me to grow up and take steps towards feeling better. It was obvious to AJ and me that we had to move in together. Maybe then we'd stay home more. Read more books. Eat better food.

***

There wasn't a particular event that heralded a new version of my life where illness was all over me, but there was an undeniable shift. It was like a slight change in the weather, where the air goes cold and the ants hurry to safety. The pressure that had been building inside me finally broke, and the first big, fat raindrops fell to the ground. The storm was finally here. I was afraid, but beneath that fear was relief: no more waiting for the inevitable.

AJ and I rented a little terrace in Collingwood where we lumped an enormous amount of our junk, both physical and emotional, into one of the extra rooms. Over the share-house years we had carried boxes and bags and books and pieces of paper around with us wherever we moved, not yet sure what would end up being important. I had dropped my study load down to part-time and had found myself a casual job at the *Age* newspaper selling classified advertising to motoring enthusiasts. It was the first time I'd worked in an office, and I loved the thrill of putting a jacket on and pretending I was almost a legitimate person with a real job. I could still hide my illness well enough while I was there, pretending that it would soon resolve itself. AJ was slowly building a plan to open his own music studio, and like me, working a series of uninspiring jobs to help pay our rent.

We shared our house with a sophisticated network of mice. We knew they were there because they became increasingly brazen, their trail of destruction more and more dramatic. I realised later that it must have been a sign of what was to come – they ate away at the very foundations of our home, and as much as we tried, we were unable to rid our lives of them. We were overrun.

We lay awake listening to the night, to the mice and to the endless rumble of cars. Our pillows rested just below the cold glass of a low bedroom window, which opened onto the Eastern Freeway where traffic flowed twenty-four hours a day. The walls would rumble and the windows would shake. Friends who believed in that sort of stuff said that having our heads in that position was bad feng shui, as bad dreams could enter from the world outside. We should have listened.

Chopper Read had once lived on our street with his sister, and we were just down the road from the ex-girlfriend and baby of a famous Melbourne footballing identity. It was the perfect microcosm of a city that was full of these sorts of collisions. And among all of those disjointed images and juxtapositions, it was the street where, I think, my slow descent into illness truly began.

Though I had become increasingly aware that something was lurking inside me, I doubled my efforts to ignore it, practising mind over matter until the banging and grunting and thrashing just became too loud. Was I sick? Could I be? Like, in a real way?

For AJ and me, life changed without much fanfare, but our relationship began to take a different shape. When we'd first met, we would talk endlessly about finding an old, run-down caravan to put on land somewhere, living there and watching as the world rolled around us. We would never settle, of course – we were too young and I was too restless to believe that – but the idea of setting sail together in our own ship would keep us talking into the early hours of the morning. 'The Lolo Brothers' was what we called ourselves, a team name that has stuck for twenty years.

As the clouds gathered, we never discussed how our life together might have to change – it all happened too gradually. It was small things first, like how much energy I had. I started finding it hard to get through ordinary tasks. My fingers hurt and my muscles would ache. The fatigue made everything feel like I was moving through poured concrete. Worse, I could sense how tiring it was for AJ to be around someone who was always tired.

Then larger things started happening, like not being able to move easily, and wanting to sit down all the time because it hurt to stand. I would need to be close to a toilet at all times because out of nowhere I would be hit with an urgent need to go. Pain vibrated out of me and I could see he felt it too: it was a shared pain that we hit back and forth, instinctively, trying to keep it from touching the ground.

This new emotional terrain was unlike anything we had encountered before. To begin with, we each retreated, me grappling with having an illness that I couldn't outrun, and him slowly working out how my sickness would affect his life, and what role he should play. And together, we were trying to work out how to live a vastly different life to the one we had assumed we'd be living.

I stopped working at the *Age* – it was clear I needed to find something more flexible. But that wasn't as easy to do as I'd hoped. Work became tougher to find because I was increasingly unreliable, and we were constantly shifting small amounts of money from one glass jar to another to make sure we could pay the bills. Any ideas either of us might have had to begin a career and build a life were pushed down deep. The glass jars full of coins and *IOU* notes stuck around for many, many years to come.

Relationships often undergo shifts, a couple pulling in sails in order to navigate a choppy sea, but they may not always move as one. It felt as though we were both running around on the deck, yelling instructions to each other as the wind hit hard and we were blown off course. As described in the article 'Quality of life: impact of chronic illness on the partner', illness is often dealt with at different rates by each person, putting pressure on the partnership: '...when individuals experience a major change (e.g. in health state), their internal standards, their values or their conceptualisation of quality of life can alter with it. This adaptation is likely to occur in both patient and partner, but if it happens at different rates this can lead to a divergence in quality of life between them.'

For a long time, AJ and I were dealing with an event we weren't even sure had happened. Our understanding of illness was something that would eventually be resolved, so to a point, we were both just waiting for it to all go back to normal. But everything didn't magically return to normal, and eventually I realised I had run out of tricks, or deferrals, or changes of subject. I couldn't hide anymore. I had to see a doctor. AJ nodded when I told him, careful not to overstep the role that he had here, walking a tightrope between telling me what to do and showing compassion for what I was going through. It was a tightrope I watched with an eagle eye, expecting him to take a fall.

***

When I first began feeling sick, I'd kept it largely to myself. There was a chasm between what I needed and what I was able to access from the people around me. It felt like the more I needed help that I couldn't ask for, the deeper the pit inside me became. But as the pain increased, I longed to talk about it with the people that I loved, and for them to help me put myself together again. By the time we had been living in Collingwood for a few months, I was desperate to have these kinds of conversations – I couldn't think of anything else.

At first, I was coy, and only half-tried to talk. I was worried that I wouldn't be understood, and so I only shared small details with certain people to test the waters. Fundamentally, it was embarrassing. I was struggling to find the precise words to tell people what was happening; to give enough detail – but not too much – to convey what it had been like.

But it soon dawned on me that it might not be possible to have my illness understood the way I needed it to be. Nobody could feel what I felt. I was in my own body, entirely separate from everyone around me, and words were inadequate to explain what I was experiencing. It felt like there was no language that could convey how I felt, and I was utterly alone in my pain. I gave up for a time, because more painful than the solitary experience of illness was not having it understood. Not having the words to tell the people that I loved what it felt like to be in my own hell. Because I still had a niggling doubt. Maybe there were no words because it didn't really exist. Maybe I was making too much of it. Maybe I wasn't sick at all. Maybe I should have been dealing with it better than I was.

The invisibility of this illness meant that I often found myself alone, lost inside my body. To make sense of it, I would burrow deeper inside while the rest of the world moved further away.

And so began a long period of strange disconnection from my friends, which I'm sure I was mostly responsible for and was aware of. Perhaps to look at us, you wouldn't have guessed that there had been a distancing, and I would be surprised if any of my friends even noticed it, but I felt myself slowly drifting away as my life became increasingly different from theirs. When we spoke, I couldn't see myself reflected in their stories anymore. The lightness with which they seemed to live, the wildness of being young, had become too difficult for me to understand. There were moments when I reached out to someone, tentatively, but I don't think they saw it, or knew what I was asking – which was for them to hold onto me.

So my little boat just drifted in this new current, unmoored from the world where I had once lived.

two

on illness

I was lying in bed in the middle of the day, wide awake. Each time I wanted to move my body, I needed to negotiate with it first, and to prepare for the pain that it would involve. So I stayed as still as I could, staring at the wall. I tried to pretend that I was no longer part of the world, that if I was quiet enough, breathing slowly enough, I might disappear.

I remembered how once, when I was a child, my dad fell down some stairs in the backyard while fixing our house, and a piece of wood landed on his back. He lay there for a moment and did a quick scan of his body. He hadn't been hurt, but he began to wonder what would have happened if he had been. My siblings and I were out of sight indoors, lying in all sorts of directions across the lounge-room floor watching television. My mum's eyes were fixed on her knitting, and the click and clack had sent her into a meditative state. We were oblivious to the fact that he was lying out there in the backyard. As the sun started to lower across the sky, he wondered how long it would take for anyone to notice that he'd fallen. But no one came out. No one noticed.

I felt like the same thing had happened to me, except I had been lying here now for days.

I had begun to understand that this illness was not a wave that I could ride, but rather one that I needed to plunge down beneath, diving as deep as I could and holding my breath while its full force crashed above me. But somehow we still had to find a way to pay the rent and the bills. AJ was hoping to break us out of the cycle of endless casual jobs by starting a small recording studio. But the money was slow, and the jars that we divided our money into every week were quickly emptied. So I measured my life in blocks of time. I'd spend days in bed building up reserves of power, like Super Mario might do, until I had enough to get myself to my casual job. Then I'd use it in one fell swoop, and have to head straight back to bed to build it up again.

As I lay in bed, I imagined and re-imagined how I might change the design of the room. If I closed my eyes, I could retrace every hole and paint chip and spider web with pinpoint accuracy. My fevers had a hallucinogenic quality, and I would wake, drenched in sweat, from dreams spent wrestling with the nature of language, with questions I couldn't formulate into words but that nonetheless had me thrashing around, as if trying to birth the answer.

Fevers could also take me in a whole new direction, where I would see the world through a different set of lenses, slightly magnified, slightly distorted. I would watch old episodes of *Seinfeld* one after the other and immerse myself in their utter brilliance. I had always found them funny, but the fever could somehow decode the humour in a new way.

Eventually I turned that new perspective inwards, onto my illness itself. I began to conduct experiments on myself, asking questions as a child might: a perpetual, *but why?* I circled so tightly around the concept of illness that I removed it almost entirely of meaning.

***

When I was little I was scared of becoming sick. I thought it would be the end of me.

I never liked the idea of doctors and I had always been afraid of hospitals. Perhaps it was a fear of the unknown, tangled up in an anticipation of pain. Knives and needles and tubes and all sorts of invasions. Hospital, as a place of torture and horror, loomed as large as the forest in 'Little Red Riding Hood', or the troll under the bridge in 'Billy Goats Gruff'.

I have a scar that travels the entire trail of my abdomen, and if I run my finger along this edge, I can feel a solid line that traces all the way back to the starting point of this fear. Back to the time when I was three years old and my appendix ruptured. Even though I must have been suffering terribly when it burst, I was so determined to avoid being admitted to hospital that, as the doctors pushed down hard on my little body, I convinced them that there was no pain. I must have believed that keeping the pain a secret, and in my control, would be better than trusting these strangers with it. Even at that young age, I had a deep sense that allowing my body to be taken away from me had to be a last resort.

After convincing them over the course of that long day that there was nothing wrong, the rupture was eventually detected and resulted in an admission to hospital that I can remember in unnerving detail.

I can see myself lying in a bed with barred sides that were taller than me and that I could reach my hand through when I wanted to be touched by my family. At the side of the bed, along the wall of the ward, was a set of stairs that led somewhere that I couldn't quite see, only imagine. There was, at some point during my stay, a visit from Darryl Sommers (it must have coincided with a fundraising event). I can still see him as he stopped by the end of the bed and remember asking him, 'But where's Ossie?' I remember a Cookie Monster piano that made Cookie's eyes spin every time you hit a key, brought in by a favourite uncle. I remember a pink nightie with a frill.

I also remember the terror, looking through the bars of the bed and waiting for someone to come and do something that I didn't want them to do. It made me ferocious. I have heard that I was so angry at my mum for leaving me in the hospital each night – back then parents weren't allowed to stay – that when she showed up early the next morning to sit for those long days beside my bed, I would painfully twist the skin on her arms with my hands, like my brother had done once to me. I've heard that I looked the doctor who saved my life square in the eye and told him that I hated him. I had never used that word before, but I had said it with such intensity that, apparently, he was hurt. I am also told that I wouldn't let my mum carry me out of the hospital – I insisted that I would walk. When I got home, I wouldn't let them put the pink nightie with the frill on me ever again.

For me to be *so* sure at only three years of age that I needed to avoid hospital at all costs, the fear must have come earlier. It seemed that this knowledge was part of my body, like an organ. Maybe it was coded into me, handed down from my ancestors – a sort of trauma memory that every generation is tasked to carry.

***

As I grew older, the idea of sickness became both thrilling and frightening. When I claimed illness, it was usually met with initial scepticism from those in charge of me. But then, when I'd passed some of their arbitrary tests, I would be given permission to be absent from the regular day. I was special.

But that idea became more complicated.

I remember sitting cross-legged on the floor of an old classroom in a primary school in the suburbs of Melbourne. I must have been very young, but every door handle, every window, every fence in that school has been seared into my mind, as has the smell of spring that would fill me as I ran in through the wire gates – usually late, but with a boiling excitement about the day ahead.

This day, I turned my head to the orange classroom door, and to my surprise, peeking through, was my mum with her eighties perm and big glasses. I was thrilled to see part of my other life, my home life, unexpectedly find its way to my school. I sat up straighter so that she would see how good I was. But her whispers to my teacher were angular and direct and she didn't smile, so I knew something was wrong.

My teacher called my name and told me to get up and get my bag, I needed to go home. I jumped up beaming, very aware that the rest of the class was looking on with equal parts jealousy and curiosity. Disruptions like these were the stuff of dreams: to be the chosen one, with such important business that you had to leave without warning.

As we walked to the car, Mum told me my dad had been in a serious car accident. She was walking two paces ahead of me: 'He'll be okay; he was lucky. His car has been crushed...'

My mind raced with the possibilities as she gave me the hard facts, breathless and half-hearted – I was not her top priority in that moment.

'Lucky' was the word that rang inside my head. What did that mean? That he might *not* have been alright? That he was nearly killed? They were ideas that had sat inside me, but until then, hadn't made sense. I didn't really understand that something like this could just happen. Illness and injury were things that came and went, not things that could destroy someone close to me. I was suspicious about it all.

When Dad got home, I was scared of him. I would look at him around corners: he wore a neck brace, and his hair was in a constant mess. There was a new baby girl in our house now too, making four kids all vying for attention. I was just two years younger than my brother, who had a seemingly limitless imagination when it came to finding ways to antagonise me – acts that I would, in turn, swiftly deal out to my next brother, five years younger than me. Everything felt moments away from collapse. Dad would tell the story of his lucky escape as if it was something good. I hated that story, because until then I hadn't realised that he could ever need to escape from anything.

This new idea of frailty in our home spooked me. I would try to stay small and keep close to the walls so I wouldn't be noticed. My parents were busy with the neck brace and whiplash and broken bones and a new baby, so it was easy for me to fade into the background. I can still see Dad lying on his bed with that big neck brace on, spending his days cuddling the new baby and staring at the roof. I didn't like him like that. I wanted to pretend that he wasn't my dad until he got better again and started acting like he should. I kept as far away as I could.

His broken body might have had an obvious physical cause, but his vulnerability frightened me just the same. I couldn't distinguish between illness and injury, and so I looked for signs of sickness in the corners in our house, secretly trying to work out what it was that had changed him. I believed the real story of illness was being kept from me. I certainly didn't feel like I understood it as I should.

***

For most of my life, until I myself became sick, I had thought of illness as an invasion by a foreign actor. Sickness was the state of being under attack, and you had only your wealth, your genetic luck and your perspective to determine how prepared you were for war.

When I was young, I'd believed that how well you could fight was impacted by your compliance with mythologies such as eating carrots for your eyesight, or spinach for your blood. But even then, illness dealt its most wicked blows to those of us who had failed something: the genetic race, the healthy-eating race, the race to be a better person.

The idea of illness as invasion can be traced back through time, right back to when humans first clustered and disease spread. Brock Bastian, from the School of Psychological Sciences at the University of Melbourne, was one of the researchers to look into the relationship between morality and illness:

> 'People often posit the existence of supernatural "forces" or "spirits" to explain events that do not have a clear biological or psychological explanation – a tendency that is especially acute for harmful events ... Furthermore, spiritual responses to physical illness and disease remain popular in modern societies (e.g. faith healing, spiritual healing), where health complaints are sometimes attributed to the will of God or the work of the Devil.'

From this base, we built beliefs that have stayed alive in different forms throughout time. Right across cultures and history we see the ongoing search for the reason why illness exists. There is a struggle to understand illness as a normal process of the human body – it must be a punishment, or a sign of disharmony. Social structures and cultural norms have been built around this idea, all centred on the notion that illness is the fault of the individual, with a cost that is also borne by their community.

In the early 1950s, one of the founding fathers of American sociology, Talcott Parsons, described illness as a deviance as he developed a theory called the 'Sick Role'. This theory asserts that a sick individual is not a productive member of society: being sick is not a physical state, but a social one, which includes rights and responsibilities. The sick person has two rights: firstly, they are exempt from normal social roles, and secondly, they are not responsible for their condition. But those rights are countered by their obligations, the first being that the sick person should try to get well, and the second being that the sick person should seek technically competent help and cooperate with the medical profession.

The sick person should try to get well. As if getting well is based on effort and choice.

While Talcott Parsons's theories were abandoned later that century, I felt I was still bumping against their ghosts. I didn't just feel sad about my sickness, I felt guilty. If I truly wanted to be well, truly tried to, wouldn't I have got better by now?

***

There was one more moment in my childhood that circled my mind while I lay in my bed. Another embedded fragment of a memory that could suck me back through the portal.

My little body ached. I was about six years old and had been feeling pain for weeks, mainly under my arms and my neck. And I was tired; the aches would pull at me and make me want to lie down. Lifting my arms hurt.

When my mum took me to the doctor to find out why I was sick all the time, I could tell he was uninterested, looking at my mum like she was stupid. You learn what that look means, early on, when you're a little girl. He lounged back in his chair and told Mum she was making too much of a fuss about her daughter and that she should treat me more like she would treat her sons. The absurdity of the proposition was difficult to respond to — her sons weren't sick.

He waved us off and told us to come back if I didn't improve. I could tell that Mum was smarting from his dismissal. I could hear it in her voice as we headed home. It wasn't the first time someone had spoken to her like this, but it was my first experience of realising that my sickness was only going to be legitimised if the man in the white coat believed in it. If he didn't, then it didn't exist, and he would be right to look at Mum the way he had.

The sting of my mother's shame was also mine. In an absurd way, I wanted to be sick enough so that she wouldn't be laughed at. I felt for the first time, but certainly not the last, the strange desire for him to find something wrong with me, because if he didn't then it would make me a stupid girl too. It was the first time, but certainly not the last, that I would doubt what I knew about my body: maybe my arms didn't hurt as much as I thought; maybe I wasn't as tired as I felt. It was the first time, but certainly not the last, that I assumed the man in the white coat knew more about me and my mum than we knew about ourselves.

When I didn't improve, we were forced back into his room. His tone hadn't changed – he clearly thought that we were an annoyance – but he wrote on some papers and told my mum to admit me to hospital that day for some tests. I looked at her, hoping this shift had made her happy, and as she snatched the papers from his hand, I thought I saw a tiny glimmer of pride or victory, I'm not sure which.

Like the first time I was taken to hospital, I can remember the tiniest of details. I can remember being stripped down and standing in a room with doctors and nurses, and being asked to lift my arms in the air so they could feel where it was sore. I didn't trust them. I watched their every move. I expected a needle or a knife to hurt me at any moment.

Dad would visit me each night and buy a packet of salt and vinegar chips. As we ate them we would push some chips through the bars of the bed opposite, where a little girl watched our every move. She would crawl her way slowly to the chips and eat them without taking her eyes off us. My parents weren't allowed to stay overnight, and when they left each evening I would watch the cars through the window, sure that I could see Mum and imagining that she might never come back.

They never found anything that they could diagnose me with, and eventually I started to feel better again, so after about a week, they let me go home. Mum looked relieved, but I wanted to do a good job for her. I wanted to find out that there was something wrong, that there was a cause for this pain.

***

You come to understand that illness is fundamentally shameful. The broken and cut-up parts of us, sometimes deep within us, either separate us from our former selves or from the 'normal' world. There is shame because we are not like others, not like we used to be. Shame because we can feel like a burden. Because our dysfunction is uncomfortable in a normal world. We are asked to feel shame because we can't control our bodies. We feel shame because some of us are made to feel as if our illness is ugly. We feel shame when we seek compassion for illness from a world that is often incapable of giving it, as it runs at a million miles an hour around us.

Before we have a name for our illness, before a diagnosis is made, we are made to feel shame because people might think we're faking it. Or making too much of it. Or it is our fault. There is a deep societal suspicion of ill people, codified in 'helpful' remarks: 'Should you change your diet?' 'Have you tried acupuncture?' It is made clear to us through these covert comments that illness can be fixed and it's our responsibility to fix it. If we don't, if we are not seen to be working hard enough, or we complain too much, the world very quickly tires and points the finger of responsibility back at us: 'So, what are *you* doing about it?'

So we hide beneath our clothing, and our skin is a secret that the world cannot be trusted with.

three

the search for an answer

The stories of how chronically ill people finally receive their diagnosis are often stories of pain, delays, confusion and multiple missteps. They are stories of vastly differing skill sets between health care providers and, at times, fundamentally contrasting perspectives, and they regularly expose the health system's wild inequity and lack of resources. These stories reveal that in our health system, the quality of care any individual receives is dependent on their postcode, their gender, their cultural background and how much money they have available to jump a queue or find a better doctor.

***

Eventually, around 1997, I realised that this illness was not going away. Once I had exhausted the suggestions and solutions offered by my friends and family, I accepted that I needed to find a doctor.

Living on a meagre student allowance meant that the bulk-billed, fluoro-lit doctor's room down on the main road in inner-city Melbourne was my only option. My friends and I had been into many of these types of doctor's surgeries over the years and definitely had our share of bad experiences: doctors who had said inappropriate things, who had been dismissive and rude, who had judged us by our piercings and clothing, or had given us drugs we shouldn't have had.

That clinic on Smith Street was typical. 'Bulk-billed' was painted across the front window, and inside was small and cramped. Posters offering access to extra health support were arranged on the walls with no concern for symmetry, and there was a pile of out-of-date magazines on an old coffee table in the corner. Some celebrity was pregnant, or not, as I scanned an old copy of New Weekly while sizing up the room. The other patients looked strung-out. Smith Street bustled with people who had found themselves on the outer. Drugs were a big issue in the area, so people with a wide array of mental health challenges made their way through the doors. As I sat, one patient went on a verbal tirade, telling the room that he'd been cheated. This sort of thing was mostly tolerated in these clinics, but when the receptionist couldn't calm him down, he was finally asked to leave – which he did, his departure accompanied by a spray of expletives.

These types of patients often needed complex care, the kind that requires the best doctors available. But in my experience, the doctors in these places were just filling the gaps: inexperienced or disengaged. This was not the sort of practice where you'd build an ambitious career.

When I was finally shown in to see the doctor, I found her erratic and overly familiar. She took a phone call in the middle of my appointment from her son, who, apparently, was having difficulty making dinner. I sat listening, unsurprised. When the urgent call was over, she suggested that I might have food allergies and that I should probably go off bread for a while.

I shrugged; I hadn't expected much more. I went home and entertained the possibility that I had been worried about nothing. Maybe it was just something to do with food and allergies? I had already tried eliminating certain foods, but maybe I hadn't done it right, or had been focused on the wrong ones? But the weeks were long and difficult, and removing bread from my diet didn't help. I went back for another game of doctor roulette.

The moment I sat in Jeff's cramped room, I knew he was different. What struck me most was how gentle and attentive he was. His face hardened when I told him some of the difficult things that were happening, like the blood in the toilet bowl, and the pain I was feeling. And he waited patiently and quietly as I squirmed in the chair, uncomfortable about sharing it all.

He imbued confidence and care. He not only made me feel like I mattered but also that he would be an ally in this process that was worth committing to. It doesn't sound like too much to want from a health care worker, but it made all the difference to me. It was a chance meeting with one of the great doctors.

***

A general practitioner doctor (GP) who knows you well is one of the most important ingredients if you hope to do more than just survive in the health system. To receive good health care, you need a GP who is on your side and fundamentally understands *how* to be on your side. A good GP will sew up all the disparate pieces, all the advice from specialists or reports from pathologists, to make sure it all makes sense.

Dr Tony Bartone, President of the Australian Medical Association, advocates for the role that GPs play in our lives. It's not simply that good doctors can diagnose us: doctors are at their best when they have developed the type of relationship with their patients that enables an insight into the care they'll require. 'It's not just your medical history your GP will be tracking either. GPs are trained to pick up emotional cues and changes in body language.'

A good GP is alert to how the illness impacts you across the spectrum of your life, including your mental health. They will call the specialist to see if the appointment can be moved so that you can be seen earlier, and write a letter that properly explains the symptoms and the experiences you've been having. They will continue to chase a diagnosis even when it seems like all avenues have been explored. They will advocate for you – sometimes in defence against your own bad treatment of yourself. They will make sure you feel as if you matter, especially if you have been treated as if you don't in all the other spaces in our community.

A bad GP has the opposite traits. Their starting point is disbelief and condescension. They are hardened and sceptical and sure that because you're a woman, a person of colour, or you have mental health complexities, you are likely exaggerating your experience – or worse, lying. If they don't know what's wrong with you, they assess that, most likely, it is an expression of a psychological disorder. They hope you go away. They can become your greatest block to accessing the health care that you need, because they convince you that your instincts are a fabrication.

Of course, this duality of good versus bad GPs is simplistic. Many doctors are a degree of both, but when you find the one who has more faith in you than any of the others, hold onto them for dear life.

***

When I'd first walked into Jeff's room, I didn't know that I was walking over the precipice into the next chapter of my life, and neither did he. And although he was one of the good ones, he didn't immediately know what was wrong with me. Still, he had been told when he was studying that the answer to any given problem was usually the simplest one. You must begin with the most obvious starting point.

And so we did. He would take tests and I would go home and wait it out, hoping that something would come back positive. I would head back to that clinic and sit in that tiny room with him and we would go over everything that we had tried.

What were the pathology results saying? Did the creams work or did that change in my diet help?

The answer was always no.

Even with a good doctor, or team of doctors and health carers, diagnosis can be a long and emotionally challenging process. It is often a case of trial and error: blood tests, analysis, waiting things out to see if the illness will change or resolve by itself. With each visit, I was becoming increasingly desperate to find out what was wrong. Every time we went down a new pathway, I would invest in that storyline. Maybe it was cancer? Or an ulcer? Or just stress? Sometimes I became hopeful that *any* of these suggested causes might turn out to be true, even the ones that had horrible outcomes, because I was so desperate to know what I was dealing with. Until then, I was bumping into things in the dark, completely without bearings.

Without a diagnosis, without a scientific name for what my body was doing, there was no way to explain it to anyone in my world or to prove definitively that it was not just a figment of my imagination.

By the end of those many months, the illness had moved quickly. I had lost 10 kilograms and had developed multiple anal fissures – cracks in the delicate skin that knifed me whenever I walked. I was in agony, and constantly on edge. Any slight annoyance felt like it was boring a hole through my head, and I was quick to lash out. This time in my life would become known among my friends as my 'angry period'. I was humourless and quick to react. It felt like being sick was taking over every part of my life.

***

Memories of the doctor I saw when I was six, the one who dismissed my mum's fears, had cause to resurface again and again. His attitude, I learned, was not as rare as might be hoped.

Gender has a significant impact on the speed of a diagnosis. For instance, one survey of over 12,000 rare disease patients in Europe found that diagnosis of Crohn's disease took an average of twelve months for men and twenty months for women. In her excellent book *Pain and Prejudice*, Gabrielle Jackson details the enormous historical backdrop for delayed diagnosis and misdiagnosis of women, and notes that women 'wait longer to be diagnosed with cancer, are more likely to have their physical symptoms ascribed to mental health issues, are more likely to have their heart disease misdiagnosed or to become disabled after a stroke, and are more likely to suffer illnesses ignored or denied by the medical profession'.

In a series called *Health Gap* for the BBC, Maya Dusenbery reported that the gender gap is evident and can be lethal:

> 'The tendency to attribute women's physical complaints to mental illness has its roots in the history of "hysteria" – that mythical female disorder that, over the centuries, was blamed on a "wandering

womb" or sensitive nerves and eventually, post-Freud, came to be seen as a psychological problem. The terms have changed over the last century, but the concept – that the unconscious mind can "produce" physical symptoms – has remained alive and well in medicine.'

For women's health, the assumption that hysteria or mental illness is a likely cause of physical symptoms has been around a long time. We see this clearly with conditions experienced only by women, such as endometriosis, where the sufferer often faces a prolonged struggle for diagnosis and a downplaying of their pain. A research paper on endometriosis from Stanford and Columbia Universities found, significantly, that its cultural history has remained influential, over its scientific history: 'On some level, pelvic pain has been believed for centuries to be the deserved consequence of presumed depravity on the woman's part – their imagined madness, weakness, or promiscuity manifesting as otherwise inexplicable cases of chronic pelvic pain.'

At certain times, women were viewed as unusually delicate and easily overexcited, leading 19th-century physicians such as Lawson Tait to suggest that painful menstrual cramps caused by endometriosis could be caused by reading novels or listening to music. Even now, it takes an average of six to seven years to diagnose endometriosis, and conditions associated with it, such as fibromyalgia, IBS and chronic fatigue syndrome, have similar cultural barriers and significant delays in diagnosis.

In her *Meanjin* essay, 'This Woman Is Hysterical', Fiona Wright details her long struggle to diagnose her symptoms and throughout the process, her illness (which she chooses not to name) being delegitimised as 'somatisation', the physical expression of a psychological disorder. Wright suggests that this term was used in the manner that 'hysterical' would have been in the past:

> '...this whole concept of somatisation would fall apart, and rapidly, if we started believing women. If we started trusting that women know their own bodies and minds as much as anyone else is ever able to, if we took care to remember the long, gendered history of medical ideas and practices and stopped assuming that we have moved beyond this into something objective, rational, systematic. If we accepted that when women speak, it is important to actually listen. Because they're not just being dramatic, or hysterical.'

***

Some of the disparities between women's and men's health care might also have to do with the great disparity at the coalface of medical research. Caroline Criado Perez, the author of *Invisible Women: Data Bias in a World Designed for Men*, has recently been sounding the alarm on an 'over-reliance on male data' when it comes to both animal and human medical research. She wrote in *New Scientist*: 'The truth is that, because of the need to test at different stages of the menstrual cycle, it probably is more expensive to include women in clinical trials.'

Along with that, there is the gender imbalance within medicine. Women may make up 80 per cent of the health care workforce, but they only make up between 3 and 9 per cent (depending on the role) of leadership positions. In the areas of medicine that have access to the most power, such as surgery, specialities and to a lesser extent general practice, a large proportion of health care providers are white males. When most of your colleagues share your experience of the world, there is little capacity for your perspective to be challenged by those you are treating.

***

Women frequently need to navigate a rocky and biased environment when they first approach healthcare providers for support. So ingrained is the bias that it is often difficult to advocate for yourself, even in the close environments of friends and family. Sometimes the people around you are helping to perpetuate the idea that you are making more of it than you should.

Pre-diagnosis is a messy time, when friends, family and colleagues are drawn into the confusion around what is happening to you. The best ones, or those with the greatest capacity at that time, will have a ceaseless energy for your unusual problems, and an understanding of the potential changes in your behaviour (the fact that you don't feel like you can grab a beer with them anymore) but generally as the search goes on, people's interest wanes. Without a diagnosis, it's easy to assume that an illness is invented, because we are constructed to expect that people might not be as sick as they are making out.

As I started to acknowledge that my illness might be serious, I found it wasn't always easy to convince the rest of the world. 'You don't look sick', was one of the more passive dismissals I received. It is a rejection dressed up in a compliment: 'But you look so good,' I was often told, even though I was feeling at my worst. My illness had caused me to lose weight, and it seems there's nothing like skinniness to signal health in a woman.

***

I got in touch with Scarlett through the Chronic Illness Alliance, and went to meet her in her third-floor apartment, a small and beautifully set up apartment that she warmly welcomed me into that afternoon. She had grown up in regional Tasmania and was diagnosed with a form of epilepsy when she was eighteen years old.

Before that diagnosis, and while she was experiencing the confusing symptoms, her doctor had been undermining her experience: 'In the space of six months they were getting worse. And I'd be calling out, "Where am I? What time is it? I need to go to the toilet." I was getting pins and needles down my left-hand side. My GP thought that I was doing it for attention. He told my parents and family just to ignore what was happening.' It took Scarlett some time before she received her diagnosis of epilepsy, and by then much of the damage to her confidence had been done. She was left feeling as if she had to defend herself against the health system. Her family felt enormous guilt for following the doctor's instructions to ignore her, at the cost of her health and confidence.

It was Scarlett who had to bear the weight of evidence: it was her responsibility to *prove* that she was sick and to somehow convince the people around her that her symptoms were not figments of her imagination. But for someone with an undiagnosed illness it is often your word against the doubt that lives deep inside the health system and the people around you.

***

We want to believe that we will all be treated equally by institutions that deal with people at their most vulnerable. We want to live in societies that regard our humanity before any of our other implicit, chosen or imposed identities. We want to be free of judgement. But the health system is a mirror of the often-flawed society in which it is embedded. Issues that are found in the broader community can be found there.

The Australian Institute of Health and Welfare's 2018 report indicated that all is not equal in the Australian health system. The factors that most determine whether you will receive equitable access to treatment is dependent on 'where you live, how much you earn, whether you have a disability, your access to services and many other factors ... Overall, Aboriginal and Torres Strait Islander people, people from areas of socioeconomic disadvantage, people in rural and remote locations, and people with disability experience more health disadvantages than other Australians. These disadvantages can include higher rates of illness and shorter life expectancy.'

Delayed diagnosis is also common for many people in those cohorts.

Linda Blout, President of the Black Women's Health Imperative, argues that unconscious bias is contributing to disparities in medical treatment: 'We want to think that physicians just view us as a patient, and they'll treat everyone the same, but they don't, their bias absolutely makes its way into the exam room.'

And really, how could it be any other way? How could we assume that the health system would be immune to the discrimination of our broader communities and structures? The real issue here is that unconscious bias is difficult to expose, and we are largely resistant to seeing it within ourselves.

A study published in the *American Journal of Public Health* in 2015 showed that delayed diagnosis can be attributed to the 'attitudes and behaviours' of healthcare providers, which is a way to say that implicit bias plays a significant role in the quality of health care that people of colour are provided. 'As a result, patients of colour may be kept waiting longer for assessment or treatment than their white counterparts, or providers may spend more time with white patients than with patients of colour. In addition, providers may vary in the extent to which they collaborate with patients in systematic though non-deliberate ways, in considering treatment options based on patients' characteristics.'

In Australia, implicit and explicit bias has a dire impact on Aboriginal and Torres Strait Islander communities. As reported in the *Guardian* in mid-2019 by Professor Yin Paradies, an expert in race relations and public health at Deakin University,

> 'The best data we have in Australia is there are 30 per cent fewer procedures for Aboriginal patients across the country compared to non-Indigenous patients. And that is accounting for where the patients live, socioeconomic status, marital status, gender and age.'

The Australian Institute for Health and Welfare acknowledges that 'chronic diseases are a major contributor to the mortality gap between Aboriginal and Torres Strait Islander and other Australians'. The Australian Bureau of Statistics estimates that the mortality gap is currently twelve years for males and ten years for females. It goes on to explain that many of the chronic conditions are associated with 'inter-related factors ... and these factors are often associated with social and economic disadvantage in areas such as housing, education and employment'.

One of Australia's best known and most deeply loved Indigenous musicians faced discrimination around his treatment in a Darwin hospital in 2016. Dr G Yunupingu was left to wait in a hospital for eight hours without treatment after presenting with complications to his hepatitis B, which he was diagnosed with as a child. When the hospital wrongly assumed, and noted in his reports, that his hepatitis B was due to alcohol abuse, his manager Mark Grose told media that 'despite vomiting blood and the presentation of his personal medical records recommending treatment, [Dr G] Yunupingu was left to linger in hospital for eight hours'. Reports noted that, 'Mr Grose claimed racial profiling may have been a factor behind the medical staff's decision to ignore [Dr G] Yunupingu's illness, which he claimed they assumed was alcohol-related.'

Dr G Yunupingu's profile meant that the story received national coverage, but it was not an isolated incident, as the musician's personal doctor, Dr Paul Lawton, asserted at the time: 'We know that racial profiling happens ... because of nationally published data ... We know it happens right around Australia.' Those assertions were disputed by health and government officials and counterclaims were made that the advocates for Dr G Yunupingu were seeking press around the time of an album release.

Indigenous Australians suffer a 2.3 times greater rate of burden of disease than non-Indigenous Australians. And 19 per cent of this disease burden could be attributable to mental health disorders.

I was introduced to Gayle Kennedy through my friend Carly Findlay. Both Carly and Gayle have worked for a long time advocating for equity, visibility and access for the diverse disability community. Gayle is a member of the Ngiyampaa Speaking Nation of New South Wales and her advocacy has included providing a much needed voice for the Indigenous experience. When I asked her about what was missing in the treatment of chronic illness among Indigenous Australian communities, she said, '[We need] proper equipment and workers who take into account the particular needs of Indigenous people and our way of conducting ourselves.' Gayle agreed that the issues are systemic and change needs to happen throughout the system's many layers:

> 'Attitudes need to change and that must start from the beginning with the training and education of healthcare professionals

from doctors on. Bring in people with disabilities to lecture and participate in Q&A sessions. Listen to patients, make sure design in hospitals etc. is done with us in mind. You would be surprised at just how inaccessible many of our hospitals are. We need to be heard. With greater access comes greater equity.'

Gayle contracted Polio in 1957 and was diagnosed with Post-Polio Syndrome. One of the most significant changes that she has seen throughout her years of disability is the introduction of the NDIS-a national disability insurance scheme intended to give people with disability the power to choose the services and service providers they need. Although it has been widely criticised for its bureaucratic complexity and its vast inefficiency, it has slowly aided in the development of greater individual autonomy for people with disability.

'The ability to have control over the equipment I need, the care I need, having the funds to afford to attend to my cultural obligations as an elder of the Ngiyampaa Nation and engage with society on my terms has been a game changer. I know people complain a lot about it, but it has changed my life and given me back the independence I had pre-PPS.'

What is health care if not the most vital agent of a democracy, which should seek at all costs to ensure equity of access for all its citizens? The Australian Human Rights Commission notes that it is a human right to have equal access to health care and that it is a government's responsibility to ensure that equity. The ever-growing divide in the health care system as it impacts the Indigenous population, women and other minority groups exposes a system-wide failure.

***

Unsurprisingly, looking at the lack of equity in health care, there is also evidence that poverty provides a significant barrier to diagnosis. Health information is difficult to access for people with lower levels of literacy and education; lower income means reduced access to medicines and health care services; poor infant diet is related to lower socioeconomic status; and the list goes on. For genuine access to health care, an individual must be in a high enough socioeconomic bracket to access all facets of the system, and yet it is the layered issues caused by a life in poverty that often require the most detailed health care support.

That clinic on Smith Street seemed to be a perfect example of this: Collingwood was a rough inner suburb filled with the vulnerable. Many in the community were new migrants, students, low-income workers and people shifting in and out of homelessness. It seems obvious that people in these cohorts should be at the top of the list to receive adequate health care, but in fact, they are likely to tolerate a reduced level of service, perhaps because of a feeling of helplessness, or a sense that they are lucky to be seen at all.

***

Having a rare disease, if we consider rarity as the defining characteristic, is another of the many reasons that diagnosis can be delayed. Surprisingly, though, having a rare disease is relatively common. According to Rare Disease Day figures, over 300 million people around the world are living with one of the 7000 classified 'rare' diseases.

The average time that it takes to diagnose a rare disease can clock up. Firm statistics around this time frame vary, and what constitutes a delay varies from disease to disease, but a study conducted by the Western Australian Health Department found that for people with rare diseases, 'obtaining a diagnosis for their disease took a long time (more than five years), and most had to see three or more doctors to get a confirmed diagnosis. Almost half of the respondents had experienced an incorrect diagnosis. More than half of respondents reported that they did not receive enough information about their disease at the time of diagnosis, and they found it difficult to understand the information they were given.'

Delayed diagnosis impacts both the patient and those in close proximity to them. More than five years is a long time to ask those around you to believe that, although what you're experiencing doesn't have a name, it is real. More than that, the personal burden of dealing with an illness that has not been categorised and treated can begin to eat away at more than your physical health. Because when you find yourself in a long health crisis that can't be placed in a neat box, or be treated with medical therapy, you are on an endless quest to validate your experience.

Zoe had grown up in an idyllic town in the Great Southern region of Western Australia. Like her three sisters, she was smart, talented and drawn to the creative arts. When we chatted about her long experience of illness, she described herself as being a sick child. She had been diagnosed with Ross River virus, but that didn't explain the symptoms she developed in her final year of high school. She found herself bedridden with 'intense inexplicable headaches and musculoskeletal pain' that no doctor seemed able to diagnose.

'Nobody knew what was wrong, and I remember Mum would say, "Do you want to go doctor shopping? Let's go and see if we can find a doctor who's prepared to think laterally and not think [you are] just a freak."' It took many doctors before Zoe found a neurologist who was able to diagnose her with myasthenia gravis, an autoimmune, neuromuscular disease that causes weakness in the skeletal muscles. 'I guess in hindsight you can really see how limited the toolboxes that doctors have are,' she explained. 'They test you for a handful of things, and if you don't have them then you've got nothing.'

From a health care perspective, it is difficult to isolate illness when it is rare or unusually occurring in an individual. And this can be in spite of the best efforts of health care professionals. These diagnoses take more time to consider, more tests and follow-ups, and health care providers rarely have the capacity.

For some, the search for a diagnosis never ends. These people are relegated to the world of the uncategorisable. The undiagnosable.

***

The reality of diagnosis is a far cry from the myth perpetrated by TV. On shows such as *House*, *The Good Doctor* and *Grey's Anatomy*, the doctor, usually a wonky genius, is presented with a patient who has a series of unusual symptoms. The all-knowing, often socially awkward or even sociopathic doctor then uses their razor detective skills and encyclopaedic knowledge of medicine to uncover the underlying cause of illness. The patient is rescued and the doctor continues in his humble quest to make people well again.

But in reality, a large number of patients are left undiagnosed or have a years-long delay in their diagnosis, and the absence of answers can leave a person feeling lost and confused. The mental health issues that build around an undiagnosed illness may well contribute to the suspicion that their symptoms really are psychological.

A report in *The Orphanet Journal of Rare Diseases*, 'A window into living with an undiagnosed disease', describes how adults who have not received a diagnosis often feel that they need to continually legitimise their illness to doctors: 'Thus, regardless of age, undiagnosed patients have extensive medical and psychological needs related to obtaining a diagnosis and appropriate management.'

Often, in a defiant act of autonomy, and to regain some control, patients turn to 'Dr Google'. When I was searching for a diagnosis it was 1997 and the internet was still a relatively new and uncommon tool, so my relationship with Dr Google didn't begin until some time later. Even so, I became acquainted enough with it to know that a combination of symptoms typed into a search engine will bring up an incredibly wide range of possible causes – from minor to fatal. Even so, we are increasingly seeking counsel from the computer oracle. Google Health Vice President David Feinberg, MD confirmed in 2019 that health searches on Google amounted to roughly 70,000 every minute and 7 per cent of the total search engine traffic. In the void that is created when there are no answers, we look to anything to help ease the immense psychological pain that being undiagnosed can create.

So common has our desperate search for answers on the internet become that it is now recognised as its own condition, called 'cyberchondria' (also known as 'compucondria'). It describes the escalation of concerns about common symptoms based on review of search results and literature online. What might begin as a headache, after online research, might conclude with a misdiagnosis of a brain tumour.

A Penn Medicine study looked into how and when people were using search engines to assess their health. They found that 'Google searches for health-related information doubled among patients in the week before an ED visit, with more than half searching for clinical information related to the reason for their visit, such as the symptoms they were experiencing or potential illnesses they believed they might have.' It suggests that many patients know that something is wrong but are too cautious or self-conscious to contact an actual doctor until it's become a serious enough issue for the emergency department.

Turning to Dr Google can cause its own problems, as it is becoming increasingly difficult for the average punter to assess the validity of the information they find. Often, answers are provided by untrained and unqualified people, but it's difficult to resist some of the claims about cures or relief, because it seems that anything is better than nothing.

Looking at the impact of using the internet as a first stop for health information, Amal Awad wrote for SBS in 2016, 'Not only is the internet one big encyclopaedia created by the global population — making much of its resources unverified, inaccurate or contradictory — we must also contend with a plethora of so-called experts who try to summarise the complex into the simple.'

But the internet has also ensured that patients who have been lost in the health system have found genuine pathways to recovery. Many people I've spoken to were exposed to what they came to understand as the limitations of the doctors' rooms. There was an overriding sense that they needed to take their health into their own hands, as their doctors appeared to have limited toolkits when it came to dealing with illness – especially rare illness.

Collette had undiagnosed lupus, but didn't notice symptoms until she was trying to have her first child, and miscarried multiple times. The devastation of that meant she spent long periods of time researching miscarriage and problems in pregnancy: 'I would research everything, and I could recite all the facts about the rates of miscarriage ... the percentages of women who go on to have three miscarriages, and all those who go on to have more than three.'

Collette eventually carried a baby to full term, but her desire to research did not abate:

'I was induced early because I had high blood pressure [a symptom of preeclampsia]. And I'm like, *Oh, well, that would make sense, because 1 per cent of women get preeclampsia.* Whereas somebody who has never faced any health challenges is not aware. So, that's why I've done pretty much my own research and I know the reality of what can go wrong.'

The health care system can be incredibly intimidating. Interactions between patients and heath carers vary widely, but they often take place without any of the finesse and sensitivity you'd hope for from two people working so closely together. Instead, as I went to appointments and tests, it often seemed like the health system and I were in a clumsy teenage dance, held stiffly apart so that any honest, open interaction was impossible. For the patient whose life is on the line – or at least the quality of their life – knowing how to have a constructive communication with health care providers is essential. But learning how to do that is not easy.

In the face of the many barriers to diagnosis and treatment, some people try to navigate the health system by sheer force. This can particularly be the case when you're speaking on behalf of someone else, like a parent or child.

The idea is that through dogged participation in your own care, researching, asking challenging questions, and checking on your health care provider's background and knowledge, you push them to follow through. The hope is that they'll make you their top priority, which helps you to shore up your odds of good treatment. But this is the sort of care that you usually have to buy. Paying for your health care is often the only way that you can make demands of the system, and have any control over your outcomes.

And in fact, if you don't have the money to buy dedicated health care, and you are dealing with an under-resourced and overworked system, pushing hard in advocating for what you need can backfire.

***

Eventually, after months of going back and forth, Jeff referred me to the gastroenterology department in a public hospital. It took weeks, but eventually a letter arrived in the mailbox. I ripped it open in a state and saw that the date was roughly a month away. I couldn't believe it. How could I possibly get through another month? I lay on my bed and cried, not sure if I could hold on.

I didn't know then that when you are in the excruciating pain that I was in, you might be better off just walking into the emergency department and hoping they will get you treatment. Instead, I spent my days in bed, trying to handle the pain, waiting and waiting for my appointment to roll around. I had been working at a call centre selling subscription television to mildly enthusiastic customers who hadn't had access to anything like it before. But dragging myself out of bed and into that joyless building and trying to manage the pain of sitting down became impossible. I told the manager I was going on a holiday and never went back.

Although I had been waiting months, if not more than a year, and still had no diagnosis, I was one of the lucky ones because when I held my hand out for some help, Jeff was there to take it.

When I think back to the person I was back then, I'm not sure I entirely recognise her. She was smaller than I am now, in every way. She didn't know about the world and how it worked. Every day, she would pull on an old pair of tracksuit pants for comfort, and these slowly became a symbol of a life lost — there was no need to dress up anymore. And for a very long time, this small version of me was quiet and she felt powerless. I wonder what she would make of it all if I could have told her what was to come.

four

two magic words

We understand the world through the words we use to describe it. Even when children are born, we wait to hear their name as if that is the moment when they will come to life. Until we can know something by its name, we find it hard to believe it is real.

And so the diagnosis of an illness, the bestowing of a name upon what is really a formless thing, becomes essential for the world to accept it. We think that illness can exist within the parameters of a word, like 'tree' or 'helicopter'. But no chronic illness can be contained in one or two words. Perhaps this is part of the difficulty in accepting and living well with illness.

In 1998, when my illness was given a name at diagnosis, I thought that I was finally seeing it in its entirety, from the front and back and side. I thought I could now predict its full life cycle and how it would behave. I was wrong.

***

After weeks and weeks of waiting, my appointment at the gastroenterology department finally came. I slowly made my way into the depths of the hospital to the first clinic I had ever been to. People were lined up on chairs around an old room, waiting to be seen by one of the doctors. I had been lost in the pain for weeks and was only barely able to participate in what was going on around me.

Luckily, it was obvious from my appearance the sort of pain that I was in, and so the nurses moved me out of the waiting room. I could barely walk and I was skinnier than I had been my whole adult life. My hair clung to my forehead with an oily sheen. I hadn't been able to bring myself to wash it that morning, because my arms hurt too much to lift. It felt as though the other patients' eyes were biting into me, making my body hurt, so I bowed my head. I didn't want anyone to look at me. I wanted to hide. And sleep.

The nurses led me to a bed and gave me blankets. My skin was burning up, but somehow I was shivering and thankful for the warmth. It's this sort of kindness, often from nurses, that you drink up, so thirsty for comfort that any relief that you are gifted feels enormous. Nurses are often the ones in the health care structure who access the 'whole patient' – their medicalised self and their inner self. They are the health care workers who are with you in the middle of the night, wiping your forehead and telling you that it is going to be okay. They see you at your most broken and attend to you when you're most unsightly. In fact, nurses have performed the most vital role for me throughout my illness. I craved their care, and welcomed them calling me 'darling' as if I was a child who needed to be held.

I pulled the waffle blankets up as far as they would go, hoping I could disappear for the time being. Maybe just for a couple of months until this blew over.

As soon as the doctors saw me, they arranged for me to have a colonoscopy that afternoon. The illness had taken over me. I had ceased to exist months before, entirely overwhelmed by the daily drone as it hummed through every bone and every sinew. The illness, living just underneath the surface for so long, had grown with an intensity that frightened me, and the fever that heated my skin and felt like an electric blanket had been plugged into my core. I had no time for anything else, no room for my friendships or my partner. I'd stopped going to classes and cancelled all my shifts at a cafe job I had just picked up. I couldn't focus on anything else.

By this stage, the fissures meant I wasn't able to sit much anymore. As I slowly lowered myself into a chair, I would angle my body in such a way as to put the weight onto one of my thighs. But I would try to do it so that I wouldn't be noticed. I felt like a joke. If anyone realised I couldn't sit, and why, it would be a horrible exposure of my private world. And so I tried to hide that it was hurting me so much, and would sit where I could. The pain was so intense, though, that I couldn't keep it up. It wasn't long before I'd stopped leaving the house.

Wrapped in the waffle blankets, I hoped today that they would look inside me and find something, anything that would explain why I had become so unwell. I quietly prayed that there would be a beast in there that they could pull out and discard like a rotten tooth: something simple that they could remove, put in a jar and give to me on my departure, laughing about how ridiculous it was that this thing had lived inside me for so long.

I dreamed of the appointment being finally done and of returning to my life. No one my age could understand how vicious an illness could be. How it could reduce you to just a shadow, a scarce image of your former self. Friends were doing everything they could, but their lives hadn't stopped like mine had; they still had work and study and the complications of their young lives to attend to.

This distancing meant that I had become silent in the world where I was once full of life. My physical pain was leaking through me and was also becoming mental pain. When your body starts to break down, and the world around you breaks down with it, it's difficult to maintain a healthy stream of thought. You are susceptible to the great darkness finding its way in, telling you all the things that you are afraid of will come true. It's easy to become suspicious of those around you and doubt how much they care for you. I was unaccustomed to such dark thoughts and so believed them when they arrived. I believed that my life, as I had recently known it to be, was over.

Being isolated makes you realise that the world doesn't need you for it to continue to spin. If ever I'd had the misapprehension that I was needed, sickness showed me that my absence would always be quickly made up for. It certainly doesn't take long to go from dancing in the centre to being shuffled to the outer, where you become an observer.

A week or two before I had made it to this appointment at the hospital, I had gone to the house party of a close friend. It was the kind of party that would go well into the night, and often we would find ourselves walking home as the sun rose. Even though my days and nights were spent just holding on, I had decided to go.

I knew I had made a mistake as soon as AJ and I got to the car. It took me absurdly long to even make it into the hard vinyl front seat of our treasured Valiant. We made it to the party, but I was in excruciating pain. I had hoped that attending as normal could trick things back into their rightful place. But it was a horrible exposure of how far I had fallen. I found AJ and whispered that I needed to go, and we slipped out quietly together.

When we weren't looking, the host of the party, one of my closest friends at the time, placed a small firecracker near the car. As I lowered myself into the car seat, the firecracker went off and I jumped a mile. Normally, this sort of prank would have set off days of fun as we planned our brilliant retaliation. But the jump caused an unbelievable physical pain to surge through my body as well as another, different kind of pain. I had tried to explain to my friend that I was sick, that my body hurt all the time and couldn't do what it used to, but he couldn't understand. There seemed little point in explaining it again. So I quietly closed the car door and we went home.

***

When I lay on the hospital bed waiting to go into the operating theatre for my colonoscopy, it had been about a year since I'd first seen a GP. A year of worsening symptoms and confusion and self-doubt, and I was still waiting for a diagnosis and to be legitimised by the medical world.

The room was full of mainly older people, all wearing the same white gowns. If you had stumbled upon this scene out of context, you might have thought that we were part of some sort of cult: uniform clothing, and each of us with an empty expression, gazing into the middle distance. But there was a thin line of tension whizzing around, making the room come alive, for we were all aware that these tiny moments can have the biggest impact on the rest of our lives. It was the sort of waiting that would normally make you pace, but today, no one seemed to have the energy.

I was nervous about being wheeled into the operating room. It was like the mysterious world that lived behind the sliding doors at International Departures. Only people with a ticket could go through. I hadn't been into an operating room since I was that small child with a burst appendix. The fear around this moment had built in my mind, growing so enormous that it had become bigger than the illness itself. I had become obsessed with what would happen behind these doors. I would imagine all sorts of pain that might be coming, and I was frightened of being so out of control.

But facing a future with this amount of pain was not an option, so as they wheeled me in, I was hopeful that I would wake up with an answer. Any answer.

Why do we wait to be told what is wrong with us? It's as though without the words, everything that you have known, deep within yourself, about your body, is secondary. Everything that you have understood it to be, from the depth of your experience, is regarded as less than the understanding you get from a diagnosis.

And after they wheeled me in and dug around inside, they found the words to describe my body to me. Two simple words: 'Crohn's disease'.

***

My diagnosis was first given to me by a cheery doctor with a clipboard and hair cropped neatly around his clean-shaven face. I remember him standing in front of a window while I lay in a hospital bed. He had the air of someone who had just solved a maths problem, looking, if not smug then definitely satisfied. This was totally his domain: the answer-giver domain. And considering how hard he must have studied to know how to find answers to these kinds of problems, it's understandable that he'd have a sense of satisfaction at this part of the job.

But it was such a strange human encounter: the two of us sharing an experience that for one of us was life-changing, and for the other was just another day at the office. We were anchored in different moorings. Each of us was keenly aware of the other, so sometimes we tentatively drifted into each other's territory – he floating into my world, sensing what living with this might feel like, and me floating into his, recognising that it was only science after all, a simple set of data, or a logic puzzle to be solved. From a doctor's point of view, the puzzle of my illness had been solved, so to speak.

But how do doctors and health care professionals learn how to convey a diagnosis? What are some of the aspects of this that matter? Renee Lim is the director of program development at the Pam McLean Centre, where she writes curricula and trains medical students on how to convey information to patients effectively. She explains that when a patient is given news that makes them emotional, 40 to 80 per cent of what is actually said to them will be forgotten in the emotional fog.

'While correctly getting a medical diagnosis is highly technical and requires specialist knowledge, delivering it right requires something else. It's about recognising the human in the room.

'I suppose we [health care workers] all try to help and we all do it in different ways. Being able to know what you go to as your helping mechanism can really be valuable — both in terms of when it works but also, sometimes, perhaps more often, when it doesn't.'

Dr Lim says doctors at the Pam McLean Centre are taught about something called the 'three-minute window'. It is the three minutes when a patient will be overwhelmed by the information they are hearing, and doctors should avoid giving too many hard facts or instructions in that window. Instead they should try to just be with the patients, removing barriers between them.

Patients are often advised to have someone with them at these appointments, but it's possible for caregivers to also experience a level of shock. This was Sherri's experience. When Sherri's illness started, it wasn't clear that something serious was wrong. Her breath was just hard to catch, though it had become enough of an issue that her husband Michael had begun driving her to work. Together they had been trying to get a diagnosis for what appeared to be a worsening lung condition. They were together when she received a long-awaited diagnosis, but when she returned home she couldn't remember what it was. 'He was saying I had tumours, and I said, "Yeah, but is that cancer? Are you saying it's cancer?"'

She notes that Michael's memory of the experience was more precise. He remembered being more alarmed at the doctor's non-committal language while the diagnosis was still not confirmed:

> 'Michael was more concerned about the preliminary diagnosis than I was but didn't raise it with me before the next appointment because he didn't want to upset me with unnecessary speculation – if the doctor couldn't confirm it, Michael didn't want to start speculating. So, we went back again the next week to the hospital and they said, "Yep, this is your oncology appointment." So we thought, okay, so it must be cancer.'

It was. Her diagnosis was of a rare lung cancer called epithelioid hemangioendothelioma, the name of which she still needs to look up online several years later.

***

'Crohn's disease'. As I lay in my hospital bed, my mind rushed to find meaning. I tried to contort those words into some kind of recognisable form. I'd heard these words before. But not attached to me. There was nobody I'd met who'd ever had this disease. At first, I tried to personalise those two words by ticking off the important ways they might impact me: would it go away? Could I have children? Was it a big deal? What drugs would I need to take? How long would I need to take the drugs? Would the drugs make me sick in other ways? Would the pain go away? Hang on, was I actually *sick*, sick? These were simple questions I might have asked the doctor at the time, but I found it hard to form the words. Instead, I stared at the brochures he'd handed me, reading them cover to cover, trying to make sense of them.

That first effort to embed meaning in my diagnosis was the beginning of an attempt at meaning-making that has continued for the past twenty years. I sought an answer for what this illness 'meant' in every corner of my life. It interplayed with other searches for meaning around my identity, and it travelled to the heart of my search for a purpose in life.

The information in the brochure gave me the basics: Crohn's disease is a lifelong gastrointestinal disorder. It is largely unpredictable, with significant variation in the degree and pattern of symptoms affecting each patient. The relapsing and chronic nature of the disorder has broader impacts on a person's emotional, physical and social wellbeing. Patients may also develop complications that are potentially life-threatening, with links to increased risks of colorectal cancer as well as the adverse side-effects of treatment.

I never really delved into much detail beyond that. When people would ask me, 'But what is it?' I wouldn't really know how to answer. As with many chronic illnesses, doctors don't know what exactly causes Crohn's disease: it might be an autoimmune response, the immune system mistakenly attacking the digestive system. It might be caused by genetics, or lifestyle, or both. But there's no bacteria or virus or other invader that can be pinpointed as the cause. This was just a name for my symptoms, one that carried a specific course of treatment and some sense of what *might* happen next. Beyond that was a blank.

Still, I was diagnosed. Suddenly, from living on the outside of the medical world, I immediately got moved to the inside, where I was welcomed. I was part of a family now. *Of course no one wants it this way,* they said, *but chin up, no point feeling sorry for yourself.*

I was given a tour of the science, and a pamphlet featuring an illustration of how my insides looked and where they'd gone wrong. I was given an idea of how it might be manageable with drugs or therapy and was cautioned about its potential complications: ulcers, fistulas, bowel obstructions, and the frightening possibility that my bowel might need to be removed – something I could barely fathom. I was given stories about other people with Crohn's disease to aspire to. And I was told that the meaning, what this diagnosis would do to me, could not truly be known.

But I was not told the real secrets of the illness. I was not told how I would come to know it. Or how, over the years, it would reveal itself to me in all its terror, in all its frightening fullness. Because when I was first given my diagnosis, I had no idea that these were the questions that I needed to ask.

I was not told that I would be tested beyond what I believed possible. That my body would no longer be mine. And how the invisibility of this illness would hold me just outside the world I'd once inhabited and would force me, at times, to hide down deep in the only place where I knew my real self to be.

***

For some time after I was diagnosed, there was a honeymoon period. Finally being given a name for my disease had resulted in an enormous rush of something like joy. Suddenly I'd found the light switch, and what had seemed to be random, isolated and confusing symptoms became one tangible thing. I couldn't help thinking of my childhood mystery illness, the dismissive doctor and that sick little girl who couldn't prove that her mum was right. My experience had finally been validated: science could prove that there was something wrong after all.

I lay in a hospital bed for a couple of days as drugs were pumped into me, and an enormous relief began to travel through every estuary of my body. The drugs were bringing me back to life. Energy began to surge through my limp limbs again. And with that physical change came a sharp upswing in how I was feeling. It was almost immediate mental relief. Only then did it become clear the impact the long pre-diagnosis period had had on my mental health. Just as the physical change had happened in small increments, I had very slowly moved into a constant state of high alert. But as soon as I began to get sleep again and my body stopped its incessant, painful drone, the anxiety faded and I felt light and happy. In contrast to how I had been, I was almost giddy.

Like figuring out how to wear a new set of clothes, I tried on this diagnosis to see what it felt like to walk around in. I experimented with moving it in close and holding it slightly further away. I practised saying out loud that I had Crohn's disease. That it was me.

Five or six days after the diagnosis, and as doctors continued to come past to tell me what my life might look like, I felt like I was regaining my old self. I was funny again. And on the last day, ready to return home, as I slowly dressed my thin body, I thought I had finally worked it all out – I had faced my desperate fear of hospital. I had found the cause of my illness and I was feeling so well now that I imagined this was how life would be.

As I walked slowly out the door, I was handed an enormous bag of drugs. At the time, it was just a novelty: a big bag of medicine that I would need to arrange into one of those dispensers that older people used, to make sure they took the right drugs on the right day.

But the honeymoon period doesn't last as long as it says it will on the packet. In fact, that rush of giddiness drained away as soon as I began to grapple with the inside of the diagnosis.

The first time I ever used the internet to research my disease, I opened an early version of a search engine and typed the words, *Can you die from Crohn's?*

In scrambling for meaning, I fuelled my fears and anxieties with long sessions of research, hunting down rabbit holes to see what might be lurking in my future, finding out what this illness had the capacity to do – how it might *really* impact me. Because the anxiety around trying to work out what was wrong hadn't disappeared when I was diagnosed: it just found something new to feed on.

five

a big bag of pills

I walked out of the hospital after getting my diagnosis, blinking into the sunlight like I had just been born. After drugs had been pumped through my body and the pain had subsided, my skin felt alive with hope. I didn't question the big bag of medicine that swung and knocked against my leg. Why would I? In fact, I wanted to hold it aloft like a trophy, to show anyone around that I had won. I was going to be okay again. I could restart my life.

The bag rattled with steroids, broad-spectrum antibiotics, a sulpha drug, an antimetabolite, some strong pain relievers and others that I eagerly placed into my new dispenser. Orange tablets, big tablets, tablets that needed cutting in half. When these drugs were handed to me on my discharge there seemed little point to asking any questions, such as what they did, or how they might be harmful, or if I absolutely *had* to take them; my life was now in the hands of professionals, and I was happy for that.

The first thing I did was find an old tablet dispenser that had small containers for the days of the week. It was thrilling to be dividing the tablets up and putting them in the tiny capsules that were marked with 'Monday' through to 'Sunday'. It was not unlike the joy that I'd often experienced when buying new stationery, because I believed that a new set of highlighters would finally put order into my life. Dividing those tablets felt like such a wonderful, simple solution to all my problems, popped into a daily digestible container.

This small action of placing drugs in a dispenser gave me the sense that I was regaining a portion of control over what had been happening to me. And it was exciting to see all the pills that could be the answer to my pain lined up, willing and ready for me to take them.

I was just like my Nana Lesley, who had been dosing out her medicine like this for years. Her reasons were different to mine – she was doing it because she had Alzheimer's and would forget if she had taken her medicine. She also had a chart on her wall to remind her to eat food. I had entered the sort of world my Nana lived in, the world where your daily medicine becomes as important as making sure that you eat.

I became skilled at throwing large handfuls of pills into my mouth and swallowing them all in one gulp. If I was going to be good at something, it may as well be this.

***

That initial rush of excitement I'd felt when the steroids flowed through me in the hospital stayed with me when I got home. The dark cloud of fatigue had been blown offshore. The pain in my abdomen and the urgent trips to the toilet slowed enough that I could resume an almost normal life.

For the first time in years, I had the body that I imagined was natural. The type of body filled with an electrical current – one that's not pain, but pure energy that runs wildly through it. The type of body that can get through a whole day without aching.

I found myself excited again, wanting to make plans that went further into the future than just the next day. This new sense of hope was a drug in itself. I imagined that I would feel like this from now on. For the first time in a long time, I began to believe that I could continue with my life, finish my degree, keep working, enjoy my friends and my partner and keep it together.

The medicine was more than a physical salve; it also gave me hope. It gave me a break from the long drudgery of illness.

When you have a chronic illness, medication becomes a central character in your life. It becomes the way you begin and the way you end your day. I was keenly aware that those little tablets were now my everything and, as in any new relationship, I wouldn't hear a bad word about them.

I was quick to change the subject if anyone began a discussion around the evils of Western medicine. Or if they asked me what alternative therapies I'd tried. I felt defensive of all the medication that I was taking. This had to work. I didn't want to hear anything other than that. I was utterly reliant on the hospital to be the source of my salvation.

My body had become a source of pain and disappointment, so I had no qualms about subjecting it to tonnes of chemicals, even if they were also a potential source of issues in and of themselves. The steroids made my bones ache, but they also made my body come alive with a frantic itch that made me want to move all the time. My thinking was razor sharp and my desire to clean was unparalleled. I felt satisfied to see a mess; it gave my hunger something to feed on. I would begin with the bathroom and polish it, focused on the tiny details that would normally never have bothered me. I would fix my gaze on the grout and feverishly rub away any discolouration. I'd finish scrubbing satisfied at the ache in my fingers. AJ soon grew to recognise this unquenchable wildness in me, and if he came past the door he would be sure to tiptoe away.

***

I wasn't interested in trying anything other than medication. The wellness that the drugs initially brought me was more compelling than anything else. I didn't care that there were side-effects or that the drugs might not work for me for the rest of my life. I only cared that there was this sudden burst of light, a glorious moment of relief in what had been years of pain and sickness.

Even if I *had* had an issue with any of the medication that was being prescribed to me, what choice did I have? I had little knowledge of the medicine I was taking, which meant little power to direct the therapy that I was being prescribed. It hadn't occurred to me that I could be in control of my treatment, so I chose to completely trust the doctors who were now charged with my health. I wouldn't hear anything against them: they were on my team now.

The steroids brought a particular brand of relief. They quickly made remarkable changes to my body, but they also accounted for a drastic shift in my thinking. It became possible to have as little as four or five hours of sleep a night and still function at full steam. I would accomplish more in a day than I had in years, and I was able to maintain that energy well into the night. I would delight in writing pages of tasks and ticking them off.

But the energy wasn't real. It was manufactured by the chemical concoction brewing inside me. It wasn't long before it started to turn in on itself, and all that energy became a dark force. The steroids made my teeth grind and my heart race. I would wake up with a surge of adrenalin at 4am, and my legs would jiggle with anticipation, wanting to get up and get on with the day. I felt like a wild animal inside a cage. My mind raced with solutions to problems, with problems that had no hope of solutions, with thoughts that had previously been hidden in the back of my mind, and with creations of my imagination. It buzzed with an endless stream that sped through me almost twenty-four hours a day.

Soon I began to tire of the intensity of this drug, how it wouldn't let me sleep even when I desperately wanted to. I began to feel angry, firstly only at the big things, and then at everything. I was on high alert to find any focus for this energy. Any opportunity I found to be annoyed, I would take. And it wasn't long before that annoyance was turned inward, and everything that I did went under negative scrutiny.

It seemed that nothing really does come for free. Living with a chronic illness means an endless negotiation of offsets and balances. What you lose and what you might gain at any one time is in constant flux. There is often no simple solution or medical therapy or drug that will solve your problems without potentially creating another set of issues. And so you set about with what knowledge you have to work out what you are willing to risk in the service of your health.

Dealing with side-effects is one thing. Whether you dislike taking a drug because of how it makes you feel is another. What your body would do without the drugs is yet another. It's a bottomless pit of risks and benefits that you constantly need to weigh up.

Often chronic illness will cause pain, which means that pain relief has to be one of the considerations in your cost-benefit analysis. Pain is considered chronic when it lasts longer than you might expect following, say, an operation or a temporary illness or injury – as a rule of thumb, that lasts longer than three months. The pain relief in my bag of medication became a feature of my life, and had its own list of complications. I had heard the nightmare stories of people becoming addicted to the type of medication that I was taking. It made me wary, and I almost felt the shame of misusing these drugs, even when I wasn't. The stigma of addiction to opioids weighs heavily on those who are reliant on pain medication. According to Pain Australia CEO Carol Bennett, 'many consumers have told us they are afraid to admit they live with a chronic pain condition for fear of being judged negatively or discriminated against.'

For me, taking one of those pain tablets would mean that, like clockwork, about fifteen minutes later I would feel a warmth move through me. It would begin right in my centre, and travel out like tentacles reaching every inch of my body. The world around me would become delightfully fuzzy. Any pain that my body was harbouring would slowly be released into the air. My mind would slow down and abandon anything that it had previously been holding in its pincer grip, and as I floated away my jaw would loosen and a smile would creep across the corners of my mouth.

But those little tablets also made it feel like I was wrapped in foam, and the world around me became even harder to reach. Like wading through one of those children's ball pits, I felt like I had to exaggerate every step just to get anywhere. My hands felt like I had thick gloves on, so that I couldn't quite grab at anything properly. And my mind had no way of making any real sense of the rational world around me.

So I would let my eyelids drop slightly: a signal to anyone who knew I was taking pain medication that I was on the nod.

Pain relief is a declared human right, but the mis-prescribing and abuse of opioids is a huge issue around the world. The Australian Addiction Centre has been tracking opioid addiction in Australia and has found that issues it causes are similar to those caused by alcohol abuse, because people underestimate how dangerous legal drugs can be – especially if they are prescribed. The RACGP reported that 'the number of Australians who died from unintentional overdoses has increased by almost 38 per cent in ten years, from 1171 fatalities per year to 1612. Opioids – both pharmaceuticals and in illicit forms – continue to be the primary drug group associated with unintentional drug-related deaths.'

People who have chronic illness are particularly susceptible to the negative outcomes of opioid use, because they're particularly vulnerable to addiction. An American Addiction Centre, Mental Help, noted the relationship between chronic health conditions and addiction to medication:

> '...the stress of coping with pain coupled with the increased likelihood of taking addictive drugs both compound the vulnerability to addiction. For many people

living with chronic conditions, addiction is an accident. They begin taking a painkiller or anti-anxiety drug, only to find many months later that they can't stop taking it. Others become so desperate to manage their condition that they self-medicate with someone else's prescription drugs.'

***

When I first met Rose, we bonded over music. It wasn't until much later that I realised we also had illness in common. Rose had just won Artist of the Year in the electronic category for a prestigious national independent music award; everything was moving in the right direction, then illness began to take over her life. Since her first period at nine years old she had been experiencing severe pain every month around the time of her menstruation, but in 2015 she was overwhelmed by a dramatic increase in the pain. Thinking back to this time, Rose begins breathing heavily as she shares with me how pain rendered her incapacitated: 'I just started being in severe pain every single day and it just didn't stop. It was about ten months. And it was so excruciating. I was living by myself, and ... I got put on painkillers. I was on the maximum dose of painkillers, but the pain was still so excruciating. And the side-effects of the pain were immobilising in terms of concentration and balance and so on.'

But the management of this pain by a number of GPs who cared for her during this time was inadequate. While there are numerous pain clinics throughout Australia that specialise in this issue, many GPs undertake the prescribing and management of chronic pain conditions themselves. 'I didn't have any GP ever talk to me about chronic pain management,' Rose says. 'Their response was just to prescribe really addictive painkillers. And really, at no point did anyone mention that they were addictive, or what the side-effects were, or the side-effects of coming off them suddenly.'

Unaware that there might be serious consequences, Rose took herself off the pain relief suddenly, after her physical symptoms had slightly abated, not realising the dire outcome that would have on her mental health: 'I suddenly stopped taking the synthetic opioids that I'd been prescribed, and I immediately became suicidal. It was the side-effect of the withdrawals.' That period, when she was trying to relieve the unbearable pain while seeking a diagnosis for what she would later learn was endometriosis, wore down her confidence and left her with what she describes as lasting trauma that continues to impact her today.

After eventually finding a chronic pain clinic at the Royal Women's Hospital in Melbourne, and after Rose was given dedicated support to manage her pain, she realised that the GPs she had been seeing were limited in the support they could give for chronic pain conditions: 'Even with some of those most empathetic GPs, I would go in there and they would see I wasn't okay. They would write me a prescription because they didn't know what else to do ... they wouldn't rush to shove me out the door, because they knew I really wasn't okay, and they felt powerless to do anything about it, apart from giving me more pills.'

***

I took every drug that was given to me and didn't ask many questions. Initially, I also avoided reading anything about the side-effects of my drugs. I was determined to block out any concerns about what the drugs might do. I couldn't see how that kind of fear could possibly be helpful.

It wasn't until I had been taking them for a while that I was brave enough to creep onto the internet to see what other people had experienced while taking these drugs. This is one of the rabbit holes I don't recommend diving into. You can get lost there for hours, scurrying across the web to find all sorts of things that you probably shouldn't find. Depending on the combination of words that you type into the search engine, you could find yourself reading scores of horrifying accounts.

Many of us are instinctively distrustful of drug companies, aware that they make enormous amounts of money from the sale of pharmaceuticals to us each year.

In 2019, the total revenue of Australian Pharmaceuticals Industries Limited (API) in Australia was approximately AU$4 billion. This has grown by over half a billion dollars since 2015. In 2013, a joint review between Australian, British and US researchers investigated how these enormous profits gave the pharmaceutical industry power to influence every sector of the health system:

> 'We located an abundance of consistent evidence demonstrating that the industry has created means to intervene in all steps of the processes that determine health care research, strategy, expenditure, practice and education. As a result of these interferences, the benefits of drugs and other products are often exaggerated and their potential harms are downplayed, and clinical guidelines, medical practice, and health care expenditure decisions are biased.'

Since 2016, Medicines Australia has had a mandatory code of conduct to increase transparency when it comes to the health care profession accepting payments or anything of value from the pharmaceutical industry. That transparency exposed the payment of large speaking and consultancy fees for doctors to spruik and critique a pharmaceutical company's medicines, as well as overseas trips. Without effective regulation of these practices, trust between health care providers and their patients is put in even greater danger.

The suspicion between patient and the pharmaceutical industry could be one of many reasons that a patient rejects the drugs or therapies prescribed by their doctor, and enter the world of 'nonadherence'.

'Nonadherence' or 'noncompliance' are the medical labels applied to anyone who refuses their doctor's prescribed drugs or therapies. According to the article *Medical Noncompliance: The Most Ignored National Epidemic,* it can happen for all sorts of reasons:

> 'Patients may need to purchase food instead of hypertensive medication, or they may disregard a follow-up test because they are unable to take the time off from work or cannot find transportation to and from the hospital. Furthermore, if healthcare

professionals don't understand the person beneath the diagnosis, they may not effectively explain to each patient the importance or rationale for a particular treatment. No matter the age, culture, or education of a patient, confusion over medication causes serious concern.'

If you are nonadherent, the health system regards you differently: basically, you've rejected the help that has been offered to you, so you're on your own. This sense of being blacklisted is reflected in Dr Danielle Ofri's article 'When the Patient is "Noncompliant"':

> '"Noncompliant" is doctor-shorthand for patients who don't take their medications or follow medical recommendations. It's one of those quasi-English-quasi-medical terms, loaded with implications and stereotypes. As soon as a patient is described as noncompliant, it's as though a black mark is branded on the chart. "This one's trouble," flashes into most doctors' minds, even ones who don't want to think that way about their patients. And like the child in school who is tagged early on as a troublemaker, the label can stick around forever.'

For me, there was a lot of medicine to manage, and each day I would catch myself remembering I had forgotten something. Some of the drugs needed to be taken before meals, but others were meant to be taken after. It was easy at the start, but soon enough, life crept in and it became increasingly difficult to maintain the routine. It may not have been a conscious choice, but technically my increasing inability to follow doctor's orders was nonadherence.

Still, despite the challenges and the uncertainties, I managed to find a rhythm. The doctors would adjust my medication, tweaking it in attempts to manage one symptom or another, and for the most part things got a lot better. I could even get back to work, and I started working in a cafe on top of a building that housed the iconic community radio station Triple R. As I served presenters who would come in to get a coffee and a rice ball, I allowed myself to imagine that one day I might find my way to knock on that door myself. Maybe volunteer. I had hope again.

six

living in grey

After my diagnosis, I began to settle into a routine that all chronically ill people become familiar with: one that, as I was barely beginning to understand, could well be part of the rest of my life. When the doctor had told me that Crohn's disease was a 'chronic' illness, I'd shrugged. I was in my twenties, and my mind couldn't reach that far into the future. But the chronic aspect of this disease would become the most psychologically challenging. How can something never really be over?

The story of chronic illness is never the kind where the hero gets to overcome the challenge and come out the other side. Rather, it is a continuing series of challenges: each seemingly unique; each independent from the one before. These are illnesses that mutate to ensure their perpetual survival, and I had a long road ahead of me – not that I knew it at the time.

Once you've been diagnosed, your ill body becomes part of a system. It will be asked to wait in rooms that are built for waiting, with other people who gnaw and pace and scratch, hoping their number will be called next. It will become an essential if unfortunate cog in the mechanical world of doctor's surgeries and hospitals and waiting rooms and pathology labs. And your body will be given a number, defined in this system by all the ways it has failed you.

Whenever I arrived for an appointment at the hospital, I would lean over the desk and tell them my number. I stopped bothering to tell them my name. Once I was admitted I wouldn't even have to speak: hospital staff could simply check the band on my wrist. I thought that if you looked closely enough, you might see the faint outline of that number stamped onto the skin of my wrist.

That number tells more of my story than my name does. More than photographs of me playing under the sprinkler when I was five, or the birthday photos from over the years that are hidden in a box somewhere in my mum's garage. That number is written on every piece of paper that has been produced to track me, and it can recall my files from the hospital basement where they are stored. Over the years I would note quietly, with some strange pride, that these files would eventually expand to almost three volumes.

***

Part of my new routine was to turn up to appointments at the clinic of my nearest public hospital – one that I would become very familiar with. Every couple of weeks I would roll up to my appointment, along with at least thirty others. The order in which our files were pulled from the back of the archives would determine the order in which we were seen.

The first time I walked into that waiting room, I thought I'd stepped back in time. It looked like a scene from a B-grade 1950s horror film, the kind set in a dilapidated institution run by maniacal doctors. The fake wood was chipped and pulling away from the wall, and the floors were scuffed lino. We were squashed together on connected plastic chairs, all facing in different directions. The doctors' offices were a tight row of temporary cubicles separated by flimsy plaster walls that didn't reach the roof. We'd watch the doctors file into them after they'd done their rounds in the wards. This was only a temporary home for them: not the sort of office that they would find themselves in permanently. They would leave these rooms and spend the remainder of the day in their private rooms, seeing patients who had the means to avoid this cattle call.

The Australian health system is divided into a private and a public sector. Medicare and the public hospital system provide free or low-cost access for all Australians to most of these health care services. Private health insurance gives you choice outside the public system. For private health care both in and out of hospital, you contribute towards the cost of your health care. It's not as simple as belonging to either side, as people flow between the two, but for me private health care was simply beyond my financial reach. Still, the public health system was saving me, and I felt secure in the knowledge that if I ever needed anything urgently, I would have access. That knowledge brought with it a keen understanding that if it wasn't urgent, I'd have to wait.

Never has a room been more accurately described, than the 'waiting' room. Sometimes we'd be sitting there for hours because the doctors had been caught up in something tricky in the hospital. There was never any point in complaining – we all knew the person whose illness was causing the delay could one day be us, and we knew we were lucky to be seen at all.

I soon learned that waiting is one of the more difficult human experiences. It is the feeling of being held back against your will, your innate desire to drive forward. Waiting holds your body still while the rest of you, the enormous energy of you, continues to surge ahead. That's why in waiting rooms you see legs jiggling and hands scratching. Bodies are animated, with nowhere to go and nothing to do.

The only way to survive the waiting room is to convince yourself that rather than waiting, you've already arrived. That the room that you're sitting in is the destination for the next two hours. Then it's time to start playing the silent games that will keep you sane for the time that you are there.

There would always be a television on, but it was never tuned to a program that anyone was interested in. Usually it featured advertisements for the sort of absurd products that dominate daytime programming: fitness machines, health drinks, teeth-whitening products. So my eyes would search for another focus – a wall, a magazine, anything except another patient's eyes. It seemed to be an unspoken rule that we would all pretend not to notice each other. *I'm not going to be here for good,* everyone seemed to be saying, *no point making friends.* Until, of course, someone in my line of sight turned away to do something. Then I could spend some minutes scoping them out. What were they doing there? Were they new? Had they been coming here as long as I had? Was their file as big as mine?

Suddenly, finally, I would hear my name being read out by a doctor, who'd be scanning the mass of seats to find me. My trance broken, I would gather up my belongings and take a deep breath, steeling myself for what was to come.

***

Whenever I think of these places – the doctor's surgeries and the hospitals – I think of them as being made predominantly of metal, because metal sits in such bold contrast to the malleability of the human body. The body is organic and combustible. Metal is unwavering and cold. Metal has the potential to hurt you.

These places are mysterious. They seem to morph depending on who is in them – which patients, which doctors, which nurses and whatever new energy they bring with them. These are spaces where we dance on a knife's edge between wellness and sickness. Between living and dying. Between day and night. And they are alive with the buzz of people, all with uniforms to tell you who's who: pyjamas on inpatients, scrubs on staff, day clothes on outpatients – perhaps an outfit to inspire confidence as they ready themselves for the test results that will change their life either way. I was eventually able to recognise, just from someone's walk, what kind of business they were there on.

***

When I told someone the name of my illness, I could always see them flicking through their mental rolodex for articles they'd read about it or other people who had mentioned having it. They'd find a way to categorise it, judge it and then attach the level of compassion they deemed appropriate.

This was often the point where I would be told about my illness and how it would affect me, rather than asked about it. They'd say someone knew someone who had the same illness, following that with a long, well-meaning story about how that other person dealt with it.

But the same disease or condition may behave differently from individual to individual. Understanding that illness is not easily compared is an important step in reducing the discrimination and judgment many people with invisible illnesses face.

It took me a long time to understand that illness doesn't follow a script. It is constantly changing, affecting you on a daily basis in new and interesting ways. A chronic illness is a chameleon that will never go away. The trick of a diagnosis is that what you think you have — the illness neatly outlined in the pamphlet — is anything but.

Usually, throughout its lifetime, a chronic illness will re-form and collapse and mutate in a manner that is unique to each body. One person's experience will share features with others, but it will not play out in the same way because a disease is rarely a solid, static thing. Factors in and out of your control affect the shape it will take.

We are set on a course through our illness experiences armed with maps that will take us only part of the way, and, depending on the type of illness and how the body allows the disease to inhabit it, much of the trek is done blindly, sometimes while dodging booby traps. Like a science-fiction landscape, the terrain takes on a hyperreal quality. It is entirely possible for you to be walking through a field when suddenly the ground below gives way. Or you're climbing up a mountain only to find that the trees become so thick that you have to turn around and go back to the start. You must have all your wits about you.

As I got into a rhythm with my illness, I began to know myself in a new way. I'd wake up, take my tablets and then pat myself down to work out what kind of day might be ahead.

Would it be a good one? It could sometimes take a bit of time to know. I would usually have a better idea after I'd had something to eat. Or how my bones might feel after I swung them out of bed. A bad day was full of toilet runs, hoping no one would see me desperate to make it to a cubicle, and a fever that wouldn't wait until I got home and sat down. But there was no use in rushing to a decision too early; it still had the chance to go either way.

As a chronic illness flares and retreats, the question of what makes one day harder than another is not easy to answer. Trying to track it so that you can replicate what you have done in the past rarely works: from one day to the next, the ways you might manage your illness – perhaps with specific foods or exercise – become the very things that exacerbate them. This chase for health, where you're constantly tripping into potholes, is exhausting.

In some ways, I found this stage the hardest of all. I felt I was living in two worlds at once – both the sick and the well. And split like this, I felt I'd ceased to be either. Living in the no-man's-land makes knowing who you are tricky.

***

My life in illness trundled along for some time. I had the medication, I was now a regular patient at the hospital and I assumed I was going to get my life back. I had imagined that it would be like that for the rest of my life: a diagnosis, some medication and then I'd be able to start my life again. Just like that. And for a while I did. After a couple of months, though, the wheels began to fall off. Though the steroids had made me feel incredible, I couldn't keep taking them at those levels; the negative long-term impact of steroids are well documented, but as I was weaned off, the illness woke up.

When symptoms began to play havoc with my life again, I had almost finished my media degree, had partially completed an arts degree with a major in cinema and had decided that perhaps it was time for me to begin studying teaching. I'd loved the thought of working in media, but it seemed too far out of my reach. I had no concept of how to take the ridiculous radio plays that I had written and make them into anything worthwhile. Anyway, that was the kind of dream I'd had before sickness had derailed my life. I idealised teaching and its capacity to change a student's life – to some extent I hoped that somehow, by following this path, I could subvert the system. There was also no denying that teaching was a relatively sensible, secure option.

It was the middle of the semester, and I had been sent out on placement to a primary school in the northern suburbs of Melbourne. For weeks before I arrived, I had been spending the weekends in bed to recover from the days of work and study. My bones were aching and the fevers had started to come back. I was constantly running to the toilet to alleviate serious abdominal issues. It was embarrassing and difficult to be too far from home.

By the time I had made my way to the teaching placement, my body hung around me like a block of concrete. Teaching a boisterous group of children was the last thing I felt like I could do. Pulling myself out of bed every day was torture, but I didn't have much choice. I would stand in front of a class and muster everything I had, but kids can see right through you. As I stood there and tried to excite them about the life cycle of a frog, I had that sinking feeling that they knew I was a fake.

And it was clear a few lecturers thought that I was faking it too. They didn't have much time for my stories of illness — one in particular. I had handed in an assignment late because I'd been sick and unable to complete it on time. The lecturer told me he wasn't going to mark it. I protested and provided a medical certificate, but he wouldn't budge. I took the matter to the student union who took the matter up with him, and I was eventually marked. But the entire exercise had wearied me.

We had a loud and passionate argument about the state of education, but I was probably mostly angry that I felt like I had to fight to be treated fairly. And beneath that was defensiveness. He had provoked my own doubts, my worry that I should have been coping better. Should I have been able to get the essay in on time? Was I skiving off?

Ultimately, you learn pretty quickly that there is not much room for your illness in the real world. I knew deep down that any protesting was in vain because there was no time and no space for me to be sick – not in the way that I was feeling it, because the feeling of it was too big and complicated. I couldn't have it both ways. I couldn't declare myself sick and also ask to live in the world of the well.

At the heart of all of this was how confusing it was to be sick but then sometimes well. Any period of wellness would never last long, and even then I could never describe myself as being in complete, 100 per cent health – rather, like a seesaw, there would be stages where my health outweighed my illness. And then, just like that, the balance would shift. Sometimes, within a day, I would be bedridden in the morning and out for dinner that night. It makes it hard to understand what illness really means, and even harder to explain. For most people, you're either sick or you're not. So it's hard to make someone understand that chronic illness is less black and white, and more often shades of grey.

This became clear whenever I was asked how I was. I soon realised that it's not a real question – people hardly ever want an honest, detailed response that places your level of pain and discomfort on a sliding scale. It's just a way to say hello. So I would lie, answering in the way that made the conversation as easy as possible.

When I was at my worst, unable to even leave my bed, it was relatively easy for AJ and my family and friends to understand what was going on. I was sick. But then I'd improve. I'd find myself able to get out into the world, albeit with some limitations – but they were things I could hide by making sure no one ever saw me go to the toilet more than once. I would make excuses that I had to attend to this or that. And I would make sure no one ever saw me go into or leave a bathroom. Sometimes, I'd be in there for a long time, waiting for everyone to leave before I'd exit my cubicle. Suddenly I'd be accepting invitations again, and turning up to class and work, and I'd seem fine. This was difficult for those around me to understand. We need people to be 'something'. Something solid that is continuous so we know what to expect. Sick *or* healthy.

When your status is in flux, it also means that you can't reliably plan for anything. In speaking to a number of people with various chronic illnesses, I found this to be one of the most commonly shared concerns. While I was still making plans, from big things like going to a music festival or accepting future work, to small things like a night out with friends, I would quietly wonder if I would really be able to get there. I knew that I was unreliable, that my state could be completely different by the time the planned event or activity came around.

As Joseph Trunzo, a professor of psychology at Bryant University in Smithfield, Rhode Island, explains:

> 'The only thing you can count on is the fact that you never really know what your day is going to look like, and that things are always changing. How are you going to feel today? This morning? Later this afternoon? What will you be able to do? How much rest will you need? How clear will your head be? How much pain will you have at any given moment today? How bad will the medication side-effects be? Planning

– for anything – can be an excruciatingly difficult task and, since we are typically creatures of routine, we hang on to those routines as much as we can. This is generally a good thing – we like structure and predictability, but chronic illnesses can make this quite challenging, and sometimes impossible.'

This inhabiting of a no-man's-land made me feel a deep tug of sadness, brought on by the confusion of not understanding my place in the world. There was a period where I rejected this in-between state. I would declare that I was well to those I knew needed to hear that, or that I was unwell to those who could sense something was not right. But both declarations made me feel like a liar. I'd reduced myself to a caricature, performing my state of sickness or health for those around me.

***

When you're grappling with your identity as someone with a chronic illness, it is easy to be drawn into broad-brushstroke ideas of yourself. But that's rarely healthy, or sustainable.

There is a huge amount of baggage that can come with accepting that you are, and will likely remain, a sick person: you can begin to see yourself as weak, a burden, less valuable to society, less useful to your friends and family. Your illness can become everything, your entire identity. A study on illness identity in the *European Journal of Cardiovascular Nursing* called this 'engulfment'.

But on the other hand, even in remission you can't fully surrender to the 'well' state, because you know it might soon give way to sickness again. So you might choose to reject the illness identity altogether and ignore it. The problem is, outright rejection of illness as an identity can lead to rejection of treatment, or any sort of management of the disease. The placebo effect can only go so far; in my experience, illness doesn't care if you believe in it or not.

The study found that a middle road is often the best approach:

> 'A more adaptive state of illness identity is acceptance, defined as the degree to which patients accept their disease as part of their identity aside from other self-defining identity assets, without being overwhelmed. Hence, these patients try to lead a life, as normal as possible, in which they do not deny having a disease. Finally, enrichment is the fourth illness identity state. Some people feel that their disease has changed their values and how they look

on life and that their disease actually enabled them to grow as a person.'

There were long and dark periods where I hated being sick. I hated what sickness had made me – how it restricted me, how it took everything away from me, how it made me look, how much pain it manifested in my life every day. I would spend hours wondering what I used to do. How I used to be. How my life might have been if this hadn't happened to me. I was filled with rage. I wanted this gone. And like the acceptance I'd learned in waiting rooms, I started to see that trying to shake off this sickness leech was pointless. It was on me and there was no way to get rid of it. It would become me for life. An enormous amount of energy was required to fuel the hope that I might be really well again, and I was tired. So I extinguished those desires and learned to rest in the new person that I'd become.

I eventually reached the 'enrichment' stage and embraced being sick as an identity, but it took a long time. A lot of that process took place during the times when I was at my sickest – lying in my bed watching *Seinfeld* and pondering the nature of illness. I came to understand that sickness is not one thing, even though the limited ways we have to explain ourselves makes it feel like it is.

I thought a lot about an interview I had seen with Jane Goodall, where she pointed out the limitations of language. In her case, it wasn't illness that she sought to understand, but nature. I remembered her saying that we stop seeing the beauty of a fly as soon as we call it a fly. When we use that word, we can only see this creature through the eyes of all the people who have used the word before. We see something ugly, a pest, because that's the meaning embedded in that word. The only way to see the fly as it really is, is to do it every time as if for the first time. Language has too much history to allow for that.

So I tried to remove the words for it all. The pain that dominated the rivers running through my body, the ache of my bones and the sensitivity of my skin if anyone touched me – I stopped calling these 'Crohn's disease' or 'inflammation' or 'sickness' or any name at all. I tried to allow them to be as if they were the first time I encountered them, without history or future.

Of course, any cursory reading of Eastern philosophy will land you directly at this process: at the removal of language, and the need to experience your life in the moment and without resistance. But I came to this understanding organically, through the desire to emancipate myself from the confines of this illness as I knew it.

Around that time, I suffered a flare-up that meant I needed to go into hospital to access some intravenous steroids. I'd booked in to see an acupuncturist that day (it was a stage when I was investigating the potential of Chinese medicine) so I called to tell the doctor that I couldn't come in because I was instead heading into hospital.

Surprisingly, his response was quite sharp: 'But you don't *sound* sick.'

And, as I was slightly shocked at his tone, I fumbled an answer: 'But you don't have to be *sick* to be sick, you know? I don't have to sound "sick" do I?'

I hoped that he would understand what I meant. That my role as a 'sick person' needed a re-examination. I realised there was a capacity for me to live with my symptoms in greater harmony – not the harmony of my system, as in Eastern medicine, but a psychological harmony that totally reframed the experience I was going through. I didn't need to be at war with this aspect of myself.

I wasn't sick. I just was.

seven

trust and betrayal

When I first started going to the clinic at the hospital, AJ would come to wait with me, but soon the visits became so frequent that it wasn't possible for us both to take so much time off work, so I started going alone. I could drift off in the waiting room and stare at the other patients when they looked away. I could pretend like I wasn't there and have some glorious moments where I didn't need to be anything for anyone.

By 1999, the fluctuant state of illness had become an ordinary part of my life. Since my diagnosis more than a year earlier, the ways in which this illness would manifest in my life were becoming clearer.

I had also discovered that if I hoped to successfully work my way through the health system, I'd need high-level negotiating skills and a strategic outlook, like I was a general headed into war. It might seem an extreme comparison, but there was something militaristic in the way I learned to play the angles and make the best use of any opportunity. It also became very apparent that these opportunities — the fleeting chance to cut a corner or to coerce an ally in the system – were not afforded to everyone. And I was keenly aware that any misstep in my navigation of the health system could cost me the care I needed.

I was always cautious not to upset the delicate ecosystem of the hospital. There was a strict set of unspoken rules, and the trick was to understand them quickly and adapt, like you might if you were a visitor to a new country. I tiptoed as gently as I could, smiling in the face of anything I felt was unfair, or unprofessional, or even damaging to me. Any strong feelings I had were carefully pushed way down. Best to not get any negative attention. Try to look like the other people around you. Blend in.

I did my best to be no trouble for anyone who worked in the hospital system: the people who booked my appointments, the nurses, the registrars, the researchers – whoever I came in contact with. When I arrived for my various appointments I'd almost give a wink to the staff on the desks: 'Yeah, I'm a lifer, I got this. I'll be no trouble for you.' It was a delicate balance, trying to be simultaneously seen and unseen.

I never felt a warmth or comradery with other patients in a waiting room. You would think our common experience of illness would give us an understanding, but we weren't there to comfort one another; instead, it felt like we were all in competition. There is a limit to the patience we have for illness: we know we must endure it here and there, but we are very sure that it shouldn't persist. So, when the promise of getting better is never fulfilled, it can feel frustratingly like you're waiting for Godot. But it never pays to let the hospital staff see that.

I would watch as patients (usually new to the game) paced the waiting room, outraged that they had been waiting longer than an hour. *Rookies,* I would think to myself and would smugly demonstrate to them the art of waiting patiently. I knew that their loud huffs and indignant puffs would fall on deaf ears. No one jumps to your aid because you are irritated by the system, because the system doesn't have the capacity to care.

When you are fighting for the attention of your public health care provider against hundreds of other legitimately sick people who are equally in need, it is easy to be overlooked. And if you are at the mercy of the public system, you have limited capacity to influence how loud your voice can be and who will be listening if you raise it. I was acutely aware that good care, ultimately, relied upon the goodwill of the doctor. So, I didn't want to be perceived as a bother. Who would go the extra mile for someone they found difficult to care for?

***

Once the waiting room has been waited through and you enter the doctor's office, you'll find a most peculiar symbiotic relationship: two humans who have found themselves at either end of a great divide, but who are keenly aware that the other is essential for their own existence. The sick, and those whose job it is to fix that sickness.

The patient–doctor relationship is a unique combination of the professional and the emotional. Doctors sit across desks in stark offices, using decades of experience to make their patients well again or manage their disease. They understand their patients through the prisms of science and medicine. They might wear suits or lab coats and have stethoscopes trailed around their necks. They know big words but usually try to use them sparingly or find other words to use in their place.

But jutting up against this world of reason, science and pragmatism is one of the most intimate human relationships there is. The patient is inevitably grappling with their own frailty and sometimes their mortality, making them vulnerable and exposed. Sometimes, thanks to their illness, they have lost jobs, friendships, even their identity. In the doctor, they see a thread, a tiny skerrick of hope that they might be well again. That their upside-down life might be righted, and their dreams rescued from their collision with disease. That the doctor will be the one to make it so.

The fundamental issue with the doctor–patient relationship is that it is inherently unequal.

Since my diagnosis, I had been treated by a doctor for whom I had great affection. He reminded me of a favourite uncle, and like most of the people I enjoyed working with, I didn't like him because he was the 'best' doctor, but because we worked well together.

Early on, I had arrived for one of our first consultations and waited for three hours, only to see him walk out the door with a present under his arm and leave me to another doctor. I was outraged. When I saw him at the next appointment, I began our conversation with, 'So who was the gift for?' He nearly fell off his chair. In a light-hearted way, I told him he'd have to be sneakier than that if he was going to leave without seeing me again. Strangely, it was the beginning of something very generous between us. We had broken the formalities, and little by little, we were able to breach the confines of our roles: formal doctor, dutiful patient. I was a student in my early twenties, virtually living on rations, and he was a well-paid specialist. We would never have crossed paths in any other setting. And though we lived in different worlds, he would ask me with genuine curiosity how I filled my days and how I was coping with the illness. He was often bemused by my attempts to make a go of this or that, and he made an attempt, at times, to wonder how it must feel to be a young woman facing a lifetime of illness. Was I worried about whether I could have children? How was I planning to make money? I never had any answers to those kinds of questions.

But still, I could never let down my guard, or stop performing the 'good patient', because we never shifted the imbalance of power between us. It wasn't that he sought that power, or actively maintained his position. It was more that the imbalance was so deeply embedded in the health system that he probably had no reason to notice it.

For the patient, the hospital or medical centre is a foreign world; for the doctor, this is their workplace, full of colleagues and friends. The patient is invited into consultations in the doctor's space and only when the doctor feels ready to be seen. In public hospitals I often waited two hours or more to see a specialist, but when I entered their rooms I could only be grateful to be seen at all. So I put myself in their hands, because I trusted that they knew what they were doing – after all, I certainly didn't.

***

Trust is what I based a couple of crucial health decisions on early in my illness, decisions that ultimately led to a serious decline in my condition and then years of difficult disease. Decisions that fundamentally changed the course of my life. With hindsight, I realise they were decisions that I should have sat down and weighed up far more carefully. I should have understood that things can go wrong, even in the places that you have always believed will keep you safe.

When you're a patient in the public system, you're also a candidate for clinical studies and drug trials. What had already been established in my relationship with my specialist and with the hospital more broadly was my huge sense of gratitude for the public health service. Receiving the small allowance of a disability pension and having limited capacity to work, I was very aware of how fortunate I was to be able to access free health care. So I almost saw it as my duty to participate in any drug trials or studies that were asked of me. In that early phase there were quite a few. To be clear, I was never persuaded to participate, it was merely my own sense of duty.

What was crucial here, though, was my trust that these drug trials would be safe. I don't think I ever asked anyone explicitly if a drug trial could severely damage my health, because that question would have seemed almost absurd. I couldn't imagine being put in a dangerous situation by anyone in the Australian health care system.

Now, as I write this, it seems more absurd *not* to have asked that question. But my passivity speaks again to my place in the doctor–patient relationship. A good patient is grateful and hopeful and receives information rather than trying to impart it. Blind faith in those who might be able to help can feel essential when you're facing a crisis you are powerless to fight yourself. My decision was based on a belief that the system is a good one – and it is, mostly. But it is not perfect and it is certainly not always safe, and this kind of decision-making is done without all of the facts before you. What it eventually comes back to are the limitations faced by any patient in understanding all the aspects of their illness, and in advocating for themselves.

It's tricky to look back on choices you made that account for later trauma you suffered, and it takes a great deal of fortitude to avoid a descent into the abyss of regret. It was 1999, about a year after I'd been diagnosed. Following tests to assess that I was sick enough to participate in one particular trial, I was told that there was, of course, a 50 per cent chance that I would receive the placebo. That meant that for the period of the trial, I would have virtually no drug support for my disease, bar one medication. But there was also a 50 per cent chance that I would be on the new course of medical therapy. And for me, two things were at play in my decision: there was a genuine sense of civic duty to participate in the important work of finding a better treatment for my disease. But there was also the incentive that if I was given the trial drug, it might prove effective. And beneath these was trust, that they wouldn't really ask me to do something that could irreversibly damage my health.

***

Not long after I commenced the trial medication, I began to get sicker. I was exhausted and unable to eat without experiencing intense pain. I could no longer go to the toilet without leaving blood in the bowl. I was still trying to get through my teaching degree and was finding it hard to keep up. I was also trying to work enough to make rent and pay bills. Soon I began to feel a new searing pain every time I went to the toilet. Fevers were a daily experience. Most days I would need to go to bed in the afternoon because the pain was such that I couldn't sit easily and could only handle lying down. But as had happened before, in a crazed psychology that appears when illness begins to eat away at you, I couldn't see just how sick I had become.

My specialist had been charged with monitoring me through the drug trial. The trial doctors also kept an eye on me, but ultimately it was the specialist to whom I turned. As I descended into an obvious state of ill health, I sat in one of the consultation rooms in the hospital and told him how much pain I was in. I told him that I hadn't been eating and that I was running a fever. He was concerned but he said he thought it would pass. And even though my body was telling me that I was in trouble, it's painful to recall that I deferred to his judgement. It's painful because I had so little confidence in myself that I allowed my own thinking to be superseded by his. Just when I should have raised my voice, I became even quieter than before. I felt as aimless and as confused as I had prior to diagnosis. What was this new thing that was happening to me?

Without a name for it, there was no way of proving to anyone what I knew innately.

But that's what trust will do. Surely, he knew more than me. Surely, he wouldn't let anything bad happen.

I think back to that time, when I installed another piece of foam on my bed because the pain of lying down was becoming too much, and I wonder what I must have been thinking. Why did I think it was okay to live the way I was? After delirious, febrile dreams I would crawl out of bed, frantic with the pain that was pulsing through me, to get myself dressed for work or university. I suspected, though I had no proof, that I was on the placebo and that coming off my usual medication had allowed my sickness to run rampant. Still, I silenced myself. I decided that I could withstand whatever I was going through because ultimately it was going to provide necessary data for the research. The fact that I was getting sick would be a good reference for the study, and I reasoned that once I was taken off the trial, probably no more than three months into it, I would return to health.

Little did I know, my disease was getting worse: it was fistulising, with little tunnels of infection burrowing through my flesh. This was one of the potential complications of Crohn's disease that I had been told about on diagnosis.

The constant inflammation can create abscesses around the anus, which in turn can lead to painful passages of infection between the anal cavity and the skin, passages that just won't heal. This event would tear my life apart, leading into a six-year-long saga that still impacts me to this day.

A month later, I attended the hospital again when my regular specialist happened to be away. His colleague saw the state that I was in and took me off the drug trial that day, but the damage had been done. The multiple fistulas I had developed would prove almost impossible to heal, and meant that I would have to go in and out of hospital trying to surgically correct them. There was no ignoring it now.

***

It's only really now, as I sit and write this, that I understand how much pain this whole experienced caused me. I have never found out whether I was on the placebo or whether the trial medication was simply ineffective for me. Either way I became sicker than ever. What my doctors didn't see when I met them in their consulting rooms was that after that trial, my life – what I'd managed to cling to and build up since my diagnosis – crumbled around me. I was too sick to finish my teaching degree. I couldn't work and was unable to make rent. My specialist never had to reckon with this enormous loss. How could he understand what it was like to be rendered unable to work, to be disfigured, to be lost?

And such was our relationship that I never told him, or the hospital, or the doctors in charge of the drug trial that I believed the trial was responsible for this. I don't know how we could have continued to function together. What would he have said had I told him that I thought he didn't look after me? Were we set up, outside a legal framework, to talk about this? Could I have asked him to understand what I was experiencing, from one human to another? Could I have made him see me not as his patient but as a young woman who had dreams that were now out of reach?

Perhaps I could have formally complained, but it didn't feel possible to ask my doctors to take responsibility; I needed them too much. So I learned to live with the consequences. I shouldered the financial and emotional burdens alone. I mentioned it to a couple of friends at the time, but only mildly, because the fear of what people would think I should have done weighed too heavily on me.

When things go wrong in the health care system, or you are in a precarious situation, money can sometimes make a difference. If I had money, if I'd been in the private system, it's likely I would have had avenues to demand better care when I first told the doctor what the trial was doing to me. If I wasn't happy, I could have tried to see another doctor to get another opinion. And maybe knowing that might have given me a confidence to find my voice. But when you have no money, and every interaction with the health system feels like it is a result of luck or someone's goodwill, you can't complain. Well I didn't feel like I could, anyway.

***

Sue Robbins is a Canadian health care advocate who has experienced health care from multiple viewpoints. She was a trainee nurse, an advocate for her child with disability and more recently became a patient herself when she was diagnosed with breast cancer. She notes how commonly women and people in minority groups – including those with physical disabilities, First Nations people and people of colour – will adopt behaviours they feel give them a better chance of accessing good care:

> 'I'm educated and English is my first language, and I'm not new to the country that I live in, in Canada. And so I have all this privilege and I walk in there, and I still

feel like I'm about two inches tall. I once heard a story about an Indigenous Canadian woman whose child was quite sick, so she had to go the children's hospital a lot, and she said she purposely put on her business suit in order to go to emergency with her child so she would not be judged based on being Indigenous, like she had to armour up in order to go in there.'

When you are also dealing with mental health challenges, as many in the hospital system are, 'armouring up' can be incredibly challenging. And those who simply can't recode their behaviour are more likely to be treated with the discrimination that is rife in the broader community.

Rose, a young musician with endometriosis, spent years in excruciating pain and suffered tremendous psychological challenges, including depression, as a direct result of her symptoms. But more so, it was the delay in diagnosis, cultural expectations around dealing with 'period pain' and the mismanagement of that pain that devastated her. The cost of that composite lack of care is almost impossible to calculate, but as she described her experience to me, having just emerged from a long bout of homelessness, it was hard to imagine that the cost could be any higher.

As Rose was about to go under for the procedure that would diagnose her endometriosis and remove any endometrial tissue, her surgeon told her that he wanted her to undertake another procedure. He wanted to insert a Mirena IUD hormonal contraceptive that, according to some research, might delay a relapse of the condition. But lying there, about to be wheeled into the operating room and not having had any opportunity to make a considered decision, Rose declined.

The surgeon continued to pressure Rose, and she became distressed at the expectation to make a decision on the spot. The surgeon then suggested that she might be too emotional to undertake the surgery at all. So while she lay there in anticipation of a procedure she had been needing for years, she was forced to explain why she was 'too emotional':

> 'I told him, "I am not okay because of this condition. I haven't been able to receive treatment until I've had a formal diagnosis that I need to get from this surgery. The condition affects every single decision around housing, employment. It affects everything. We can't cancel it." I had to fight with him to go under in the first place. And I thought, you know, in hindsight, I probably shouldn't have gone into the operating

theatre without advocating more for myself to get another staff member or someone to mediate between me and the surgeon, to ensure that that paperwork was done properly. But I was just so stressed and exhausted. I fought verbally as much as I could by myself, and I went under not knowing if he was going to follow my wishes.'

The surgeon did follow her wishes, but it compounded a real sense for Rose that she had to fight to be heard. Rose had been typified as the hysterical woman, who in an extraordinarily vulnerable moment in her life had to explain how the illness had rendered her in desperate need of health support. This, coupled with years of pain mismanagement, left her with serious trust issues when it came to health workers.

I asked her if she made a complaint about any of it:

'It never occurred to me to make a formal complaint to the hospital about the surgeon. At the time, I felt completely disempowered, and all my energy was focused on physically recovering from the major surgery, and where I might sleep next. I made sure to have someone with me for every subsequent follow-up appointment at the hospital, though, just in case something similar might happen again, and verbally told the head of surgery about it.'

***

While much contemporary medical ideology and clinical practice is being developed around a person-centred clinical model and 'whole patient care', how realistic is it to expect patients to execute true autonomy? While allowing a patient to make decisions about crucial aspects of their health care is essential, not only legally but morally, how are those decisions influenced?

According to the 'Australian Commission on Safety and Quality in Health Care', person-centred care 'is care that is respectful of, and responsive to, the preferences, needs and values of the individual patient'. 'It involves seeking out and understanding what is important to the patient, fostering trust, establishing mutual respect and working together to share decisions and plan care.'

But largely, in making any decision a patient relies on information disseminated via a health care provider, who interprets the often impenetrable medical language. And because, in most cases, the patient requires the doctor to decode the data and translate the medical speak, the patient is then placed into a relationship that is reliant, fundamentally, on trust.

Perhaps there is no way around this, but it leaves the patient without direct access to information and little to go on but their own instinct. There are few avenues for a patient to weigh up their doctor's trustworthiness, particularly in the public system. Nonetheless, they often enter this relationship with the untested assumption that the doctor is esteemed and reliable by virtue of their profession.

***

During the late 18th century, hospitals emerged as places to treat underprivileged patients. Doctors, who had previously been seen as service providers to those who could pay their fees, now found themselves providing medical treatment for a traditionally more passive population. The hospital became the cornerstone of medical care, and along with the rapid growth in knowledge and surgical skills during this time, a new form of medicine developed that focused not on the symptom, but rather on the accurate diagnosis of a pathological lesion inside the body – the biomedical model of illness.

This new theory suggested that the symptom was no longer the illness, but instead indicated the absence of a particular pathology. This new model required the examination of the patient's body and the expert clinical and anatomical knowledge possessed by the doctor to formulate a diagnosis. The patient became dependent.

***

For trust to be earned, there must be some kind of exchange. The patient expects the doctor to understand their condition in the context of them as a whole person. That context can include whether we hope to have children, whether we have someone to care for us at home, whether we are dealing with other illnesses. Knowledge is not quite enough.

This came home to me as my health declined following the drug trial, when I was introduced to a new medical practitioner, a surgeon. Here I was again, with the threat of knives and needles and invasions. The only solution to the fistulas that had formed was multiple surgeries. The painful tunnels in my body had to be stitched up, covered with skin grafts and forced to heal one by one, bit by bit.

Just before each surgery, lying in the holding bay before being wheeled into theatre, the surgeon – a rock star in this hospital's hierarchy – would pick out my file from the tray at the end of the bed. He would scan it and mumble some of the details of what might be ahead, and

I would try to look like the sort of person he'd be interested in keeping alive.

I thought of surgery almost as a magic world where you were neither alive nor dead – a pause on your life. And as I went into The Nothingness, this person, the surgeon, would hold my very existence in his hands.

So how could he be so blasé? This is one of the shocking incongruities in the doctor–patient relationship. You discuss being unnaturally rendered unconscious and then cut open by another human as if you were buying a loaf of bread. The unspoken rule of this exchange is that you are not permitted to act with unbridled desperation or fear. You are required to behave as if nothing of real concern is about to happen. And you are certainly not allowed to act on any impulse to grab their face between your hands, hold them close to you and whisper in their ear, 'Please, this is your moment to shine.'

As he continued to scan the file, I would try to make scintillating small talk, the sort of small talk that might spark a friendship of sorts. This brand of small talk has helped me to develop many friendships over the years: some deep and long-lasting, like with Sassy and Josh who used to own the cafe down the road; some more casual, like with Brenda who sells me bread, or Lisa who pours beer at my local bar. I had hoped that the forming of a bond, even a flimsy one, built on the strength of some weak dad jokes, would give me a small amount of life insurance. Of course, the surgeon probably didn't need the incentive of a real relationship to keep me alive – this was his profession after all – but I always felt I would be safer if he actually cared beyond his professional responsibility.

So I would try to charm him into some sort of human-like exchange with me. But he was uncrackable. His moustache never even twitched. I eventually complained to one of my gastroenterologists about the lack of repartee with the surgeon, and he shook his tired head at me: 'It's like when you take your car to get fixed. Do you want your mechanic to be nice and laugh at your jokes, or do you want him to be a good mechanic?'

To which I replied, 'But I'm not a car.'

And I'm not a car. I was vulnerable and scared and I wanted him to laugh at my jokes so that I would know that *he* knew that I wasn't a car.

eight

the body public

After the failure of the drug trial, my illness grew with an increasing intensity. Like a fire feeding on a dry forest floor, it began travelling at speed and carved holes and channels throughout my body. What had been a relatively contained disease when I was first diagnosed, had travelled down and formed fistulas throughout my perianal area, including my vagina.

As a child, and then as a teenager, I had always kept my body secret. While other girls threw their clothes off in the change rooms after sport, I would creep into a cubicle and lock the door. I did the same at the public pool. My body was a secret.

This latest attack by my illness threatened to expose my body to the world. The disease was savaging the regions of the body that we are not permitted to speak of, the places we hide from public view: the parts that have long been treated as shameful, both politically and culturally. It felt like it had made a grand assault on me as a singular, separate and private being.

And the horror of the pain, as infection grew and oozed out of me at such a rate that I had to wear maternity pads every day, brought with it a profound feeling of self-disgust. A disgust with a body that I believed I needed to apologise for, especially if people noticed something wasn't quite right or enquired into my health. 'Sorry for the detail,' or 'Sorry you had to hear that.' 'Sorry, I'm a bit of a mess at the moment.' 'Sorry, this is awkward, but I can't sit down very easily.'

When you have a chronic illness, you are constantly moving with the tectonic shifts beneath you. And you adapt to these changes, solving the problems that you are presented with but not always knowing how the disease is shifting inside you, how you quietly regard your new self with an overlay of pain. I would wave off any thoughts about my changing body that I had internalised from a society that only viewed certain bodies as beautiful. Who cared that people may have found me disgusting? But a disparaging voice inside me kept growing. 'You are revolting,' it would spit.

The searing pain of the fistulas was a constant reminder of the invasion. The pain was so profound that every movement needed to be negotiated, but I kept it as secret as I could. I was too afraid of the questions that would follow if anyone saw I was suffering. 'Where is it? Why is it?' I learned how to catch the pain each time it knifed me, stopping before I unintentionally reacted.

For me, dealing with the pain became about diffusing it throughout my body and being forever *en garde* for the next attack. But the concentration it required left little room or emotional space for anything else. I was standing on the edge of a cliff, high on my tippy toes, aware that any small breeze would knock me over and into the dark abyss below.

I did everything I could to hide my pain from all the strangers around me, because I believed the truth was too horrible. I can remember going to vote at an election while AJ was at work. I was alone, weak and in constant pain, and dreading having to drive my large 1968 Valiant to the nearest polling booth. But I didn't want to ask anyone for help. So I lay in bed and gave myself an hour to build up strength, then managed to drive that enormous car to my destination – but couldn't find a park. After driving around and around in circles, I eventually had to park some distance away. I remember the people who stopped to look at me as I hobbled slowly up the street. The pain I was in was obvious and disconcerting. It took me at least half an hour to make it to the door, but I refused to ask for help. And after watching the opposition to my political interest take the stage and deliver a victory speech, I realised perhaps I should have just stayed in bed and paid the fine.

***

After my diagnosis, when I had plunged into the internet to find out how this disease might surprise me, I hadn't encountered much discussion of fistulas. Instead, the potential development of my illness that horrified me the most was the possibility that my bowel would become so diseased that I would require a colostomy bag. I made a quiet prayer that as long as I didn't have to have a colostomy bag, I would be good natured about the rest of the disease.

But the fistulising capacity of the disease is something that I didn't prepare for. So I was caught off guard. I had no idea how this was going to end or if it ever would. In order to be chronic, an illness must constantly evolve and find new and creative ways to manifest itself. Its surprise attacks leave you smarting not only from the injuries themselves, but from the realisation that it has whole arsenals you aren't aware of. You are never safe. If it can devastate you once, what reason would it have to hold off in the future?

I felt a sense of defeat at the thought of the endless energy I would need in order to make it through each future ambush. How could I survive if the disease continued to change the rules? I felt as though it wanted this: it wanted to force me into this grand humiliation. It was an enormous sense of betrayal. Knowing that your illness comes from some virus that lives outside your body means your counterattack is clear. It is focused on an external enemy. But my body was literally attacking itself. I was both the perpetrator and the victim. The changed body can confuse your identity, and in my case, my body had become insistent that it would control what was possible in my life and how I would interact with the world beyond me.

***

Correcting the fistulas and the damage they were causing required an intense regime. Firstly, there was dealing with the abscesses that were eating away at the thin films of skin around them. Then, when they were gone, there were the trails and pockets and holes they left behind, which needed surgery. Every couple of weeks, I would go under a general anaesthetic so my uncrackable surgeon could assess the extent of the damage and attempt to clear some of the infection away. Then at certain junctures, when the abscesses had healed, skin grafts were placed over the damaged areas to force them to heal too.

I spent a lot of time in hospital, and what was abundantly clear was that my body had become a specimen. Big groups of medical students would file into my room, gather around my bedside and observe me with an equal measure of fear and fascination, as if I was perched atop a Petri dish. I would lie there quietly, mostly naked, as they inspected the damaged parts. The doctor boss would encourage them not to be shy and to step forward into this sacred area, a space that was usually kept hidden.

For the trainee doctors, this processional was as much about acquiring the confidence to enter this space as it was about learning the oddities of my illness. The students needed to learn that this was now *their* space too. My body was their space, and this was an opportunity to rid themselves of any socialisation that suggested otherwise. At first, they would look at me warily, almost apologetically. I could tell some of them were imagining themselves in the same position, quietly praying that they would never end up like this, naked and under inspection by a group of medical students.

Soon enough, though, they would relax and become lost in the instruction that my body offered. They scribbled notes onto a pad, and suddenly it was as though I was not there at all. Just like that, my body became an answer in a medical exam, an essay topic for bonus points. At some stage during the examination, one of the students would be chosen to put on medical gloves and touch me. There were never volunteers. It's hard to describe the horror of being examined by a student who is being examined by their supervisor. Like two awkward strangers stuck in a lift, we tried to look anywhere but at each other.

Gayle Kennedy, a member of the Ngiyampaa Nation who was diagnosed with post-polio syndrome, had similar experiences during medical examinations:

> 'Doctors and other medical professionals must do more to recognise our humanity and not just our symptoms. Many of us have been used as teaching tools without our consent and have been unknowingly ushered into theatres with other doctors and students present and been made to feel like we are some kind of circus exhibition. This all under the guise of "treatment."'

A study conducted with medical students from the University of Newcastle in New South

Wales looked into the teaching of 'intimate physical examination skills', and found it lacking:

> 'Given the strength of the cultural rules about physical contact present in even a seemingly relaxed Western culture, it might be *expected* that students learning physical examination techniques would find performing physical examination uncomfortable. This would be even more so for learning the skills of genital, breast and rectal examination. There is little overt recognition of this difficulty in medical culture in general, or in medical training in particular. Therefore students are often left unaided to deal with the difficulties they encounter but may not understand at a conscious level.'

The study found that:

> 'A number of participants said that on most occasions they had little idea of what they should be doing or looking for in intimate physical examinations, and stated that they hoped that by the time they had done a number of examinations that this would become clearer for them. Some commented that tutors often seemed to have "forgotten what it's like not to know", or assumed that students had already been

taught what to look for and what their findings meant.'

I was conscious of their discomfort. I would twist my head and smile limply to let them know that I was not hostile. I had given up the fight to keep my body to myself and silently agreed to the terms of our exchange. I had developed a way to understand what was happening and, in an act of survival, deliberately closed down the expressway that lead from my body to me.

There's a secret thread running between the self that lives somewhere deep inside and the body that lives in the outside world. One little snip, and I had separated them. There was no way around it. My body had become too painful to own. It stopped being *my* body, and became just a cumbersome attachment, rude and antisocial. It was a body that I tried hard to avoid.

***

Understanding our experience of the body as it interacts with the world is essential in any discussion of identity.

We grapple with this connection between body and self when we are babies. As soon as we see ourselves in the mirror and recognise that we are who we are, we begin the journey as a separate human. Before that, we're rolling around in the world believing that everyone we love is us and we are them. Once we do see ourselves as caught within a body, with a nose and with a wisp of hair, we spend the rest of our lives trying to sculpt and adorn it so that it might reflect our true selves.

The degree to which we allow the world outside to influence how we experience our bodies is a battle that we are always fighting, both personally and culturally. The world outside tells us from such an early age whether we are acceptable. As Gabe Moses described in his article, 'How Internalised Ableism Affects my Self Image':

> 'It's hard to separate wanting to love ourselves for who we are, as we are, from the thoughts we know that certain people will have about us if we do. If we give in and embrace our disabled bodies, including all the parts of them that are most off-putting to abled people, will the rest of the world ever see us as valid, as desirable, as worthy of love and of being valued as human beings?'

We have become so closely aligned with our bodies that they become a shorthand expression of who we are, one full of inaccuracies and mistruths. But as much as we seem to understand that this has been built in a world constructed by the able, we continue to perpetuate the myth. And as much as we might try to fight it, we are often forced to present the most 'tolerable' version of our physical selves to the world.

When you're taught that your external self *is* you, then any view of it as 'damaged' or 'disfigured' or 'abnormal' is considered a reflection of a damaged or disfigured self.

In one way, the constant viewing of my naked body by health professionals, the sense that it was now the focus of a workforce, could be seen as an extension of that first day when I saw myself in the mirror – when I wrongly believed, as a child, that I was not one with the world around me and that in fact I was separate and functional. What was also at play was how utterly vulnerable I felt. I would work hard to remove from my mind the worry that these medical professionals were judging my naked body. How could they claim to be objective just because this naked body was being viewed through the prism of science? What superpower did they have that made them distinct from the rest of society? Were they not just women and men who spent their own lives getting haircuts or watching their diets or working out at the gym to lose those extra 5 kilograms? How could they suddenly suspend a natural criticism of me?

And while in one breath I was mortified that my body was being scrutinised at such close and clinical proximity, in another breath I was able to join the medical students in thinking of a body simply as a product of biology. As students rolled in and out, I was able to float away and detach myself. My body existed, but I was somewhere else. The me that lived down deep beneath my skin had left the scene a long time ago. When doctors described how they would operate or treat me, I would imagine it happening somewhere far away to a body that didn't belong to me.

***

We all long for our bodies to be trustworthy. They are the carriages in which we hurtle through the world, and if they have even the smallest dysfunction, we quickly become aware that they might not keep us on the road. So we hold on tight, with white knuckles, knowing there is a fair chance that there will be disaster somewhere up ahead. When your body becomes unreliable – or, worse still, an agent acting against its own survival – where does that leave your relationship with it?

I'm not sure if there was an exact moment when I shut down any longing that my body might somehow be thought of by others as 'normal', or that it might ever be looked on fondly or that I might trust it to keep me safe. It seems we all have the capacity to feel this way. When we are no longer able to meet the expectations of the world outside us, we can adopt some very negative views of our physical selves. So persistent is the policing of the human body in Western culture, spurred on by the media, that any deviation from what is considered 'the norm' can force us into a complicit self-disgust. In these cases, the most obvious solution is usually to disassociate. Like abandoning a car that has broken down in the middle of nowhere, you decide to cut your losses.

My body had become a weight. Lifting it up and taking it with me everywhere, day after day, became a painful burden. Now that I was fully aware of its betrayal, how could I willingly carry it around as though I was proud of it? It was a constant, inescapable reminder of its own failure.

Beth Darnall, a researcher and pain-management specialist at Stanford Health Care explained in *The Paper Gown* article 'Chronic Illness Can Make It Hard to Trust Your Body':

> 'It's very complex. There can be anger toward oneself and one's body for failing the person or for being the obstacle that's not allowing them to have the life they wanted. There can also be a lot of loss

involved, especially if it's a new diagnosis and the person is unable to do the things they used to.'

Collette had dreamed of having a family her whole life, and she always assumed she would be able to have children, but after a number of devastating miscarriages, she didn't know if she would be able to trust either the medical treatment being offered to her, or her body:

'I just didn't trust my body anymore, particularly because the first massive failure was around this fundamental purpose as a woman ... You just take it for granted that if you want to have a family, you're going to have a family. And because I had always been well, it was a massive shock that my body wasn't doing what it was meant to do. From there, it was like when something bad happens, you are convinced that something bad is going to happen again. I think because my body had let me down so many times, I just had a belief that it could continue to let me down – and it bloody still lets me down on so many levels.'

In my case, I felt I had no option but to distance myself from my body. Cut myself off. Divorce. And a divorce of the most acrimonious type. The kind where you hope that the split will render your separate part entirely bereft, so it will finally realise that it has done the wrong thing and beg for your forgiveness. When I was alone and able to inflict the most savage attacks, I would tell my body quietly, but with ferocity, that it was indeed ugly.

***

One of the quirks of illness is that depending on the medication and your disease profile, it can be a time of great weight loss or great weight gain. One of the most scrutinised aspects of a human body is the amount of weight that it carries.

I have had both kinds of weight changes: steroids have many side-effects, one of which is fluid retention. There was a time when the fluid retention, and the way the steroids affected my skin — breeding pimples and giving it a deathly pallor — made people I loved jump back in horror. I've shown new members of my family photos of me when I was highly reliant on steroids, and they couldn't hide their shock, covering their mouths and stifling laughter. I didn't have much choice but to join in. I was pretty ugly.

Once, a nurse who was wheeling me into the theatre announced to everyone that I was one of the fatter Crohn's disease patients she'd seen. That was a compliment in her mind, but it was roundly humiliating. I almost felt like I had to explain myself. *I'm sick, I promise, it's just that the drugs make me a bit fat ...*

But there is also the entirely opposite experience, when illness causes great weight loss, as it did when I was struggling to eat. With great weight loss comes a barrage of compliments from the people in your life who can't believe how well you're looking, because wellness and thinness are so often aligned. 'I'm actually really sick,' I would sometimes feebly explain. 'It's just that I haven't eaten properly in a couple of weeks.'

***

At the time, in an act of rebellion against all the ways I felt judged, I created a new game. Whenever I was on the tram, I would pick someone out, someone far enough away that they wouldn't notice me looking at them. I would wonder how they might be seen by people in their lives, and I would pretend that I loved them – perhaps like their mum did, or their partner or their child. I would look long and hard, trying to see them with tender eyes, the way we should all, always be seen.

nine

unseen

A year after the medical trial, it was becoming clear that the doctors were running out of options to fix the fistulas. The amount of time that I was spending in the hospital had reached the levels of a part-time job, and the longer it went on, the more harried I became. I was like the frayed edge of a wire, buzzing around trying to find a way to ground. And not knowing what would come next or how this would end was suffocating.

Chronic illness is a state of uncertainty, to the point that I sometimes think that's what I should have been diagnosed with: chronic uncertainty. Because from the moment I first started getting sick, I would never be sure of anything. There is no choice but to get comfortable with a deep state of discomfort – not only physical, but also mental.

The house we were living in had a rental increase we couldn't afford, so AJ and I moved into a small terrace in North Carlton opposite a high school, and I virtually hid there, wondering when my life would get back on track. During this time, the pain was like an electrical current that hummed through every sinew, and would kick in every now and then with a bolt that made me jump in fright. It took my breath away.

Our tiny bedroom at the end of a narrow set of stairs was the only place I felt a small amount of relief. I slept under a window, through which, on clear nights, I could see the moon. We installed a portable television so that I could watch TV as I lay in bed. I remember feeling like I was in a turret, apart from the world. AJ would bring meals up and try to make it as comfortable as possible. He was working casual jobs and teaching himself everything he was going to need when he eventually opened up his own recording studio. By this stage, he needed to care for me on a more full-time basis. I needed my medication brought to me, he would drive me wherever I needed to go and would keep me company up in the turret, trying to make me laugh, until it hurt too much and I would make him stop. I wanted our lives to continue as much as possible, so I would insist he go out at night with our friends when we had promised we would, and I would wake up when he got home, desperate to know what had happened – had anyone asked about me?

During the day, I would hear kids from the high school sneak down the laneway that ran beside the house to smoke cigarettes. I dreamed of being them, of living a life that seemed so simple and so free. I couldn't help but wonder how my own life had departed from that point so drastically. I was only twenty-five – how had I found myself so far from those school kids?

I'd spend hours lying there, utterly relieved not to have to stand or sit. I barely needed any entertainment because the time could be filled by that relief alone.

It was the first time I had experienced pain that lasted this long. Before this time, pain had been measured in weeks, but by this stage it had been months, and I had a small insight into what it must be like to live with pain that becomes your constant companion. When pain cannot be soothed, every ounce of you needs to focus on holding it at bay. It feels like if you take your eye off it, even for a moment, you will be consumed. And while you're trying to keep it at bay, small things have the capacity to pull you down into darkness. It feels as if you have no strength left to handle even the tiny inconveniences. You're quick to spark.

Pain that cannot be subdued needs to somehow be accepted. Any resistance will only make it madder. So you soon learn to be quiet around it, so as to not make it more powerful. Instead of making loud noises, I just grew quietly ferocious, and increasingly angry with anyone who got too close. It enraged me to have conversations with some friends who couldn't come close to understanding the experience I was having. I don't know why I was so mad, because there was virtually nothing they could have done to satisfy me at that point. But the pain reduced my capacity to deal with a feeling of distance that might have otherwise been manageable.

No matter what the doctors tried, the infection seemed impossible to clear away. When I was first diagnosed a couple of years earlier, I could not have foreseen that I was going to find myself here. Even when the fistulas were discovered, I hadn't understood that they could cause such trauma. What had once seemed so straightforward had caused my life to collapse around me.

But the rent had to be paid, so somehow I would need to roll out of bed, find a brush to try and smooth my hair, and present myself as a whole person. I had a job in a primary school as a classroom assistant, working with a couple of kids who had qualified for education assistance. They were beautiful, but they needed me to be totally focused on them and it took every ounce of my energy. When I look back now, I can't imagine how I did it. People around me knew I was unwell, that I was unravelling, and it was certainly a time when I encountered deep compassion from close friends. Some of the very special people in my life could see that I was out to sea and didn't know how to get back, and even if they hadn't had this particular experience, they knew what it was like to be lost. We have all been lost at some point.

Still, trying to convince the lecturers at university that I was sicker than I looked was always difficult. University was a place where some students would try to get away with as much as they could, so lecturers often started with the assumption that you were lying. Having an invisible illness means that you are constantly proving your illness to the world. It is not enough to show them medical certificates, they must see the pain that you are in. How else would they believe what you have to say?

As my body battled the constant infections, fevers would keep me up late at night as they broke and soaked the pillow. They lived with me through the days while I tried to work, shivering with cold. A couple of times I went to hospital just so they could help me manage these fevers. I felt like clinging to medical staff's lab coats and begging them to let me stay, to please look after me.

To add insult, they needed to increase the intervention in the perianal area. During one of my regular six-weekly procedures under general anaesthetic, the surgeon stitched in some drainage tubes in an attempt to drain the ever-growing abscesses and infections. I woke up and felt them immediately. Not only was the whole area still in constant pain, it now felt like a knife was being pressed into each wound. For the second time in my life, I couldn't sit down properly. They were a huge invasion of this private space in my body, and now everything I had planned to do would need to be carefully thought out.

It felt like I was crumbling, but there was no clear guidance on how I was supposed to deal with it. No one I knew had been through something like this. How could I keep my life together in one way, when it was clearly falling apart in another? I had to keep working; I had to pay rent. I had to keep attending classes and handing in assignments at university or I was going to fail. I had no idea how I was supposed to keep going like this, but equally, I had no idea how I could stop.

I couldn't get out of the grey space. I had not entirely removed myself from the world of the well, and so could not be considered sick. And even if I wanted to, I couldn't dive face-first into the sick world because I had bills to pay and I had to keep turning up to classes at university.

During this time, while working at an after school-care program in an inner-city school, a drainage tube came slightly loose and the stitch that was holding it in place came apart. Not only was it incredibly painful, but there was now a large amount of blood coming from the site. As I stood in the middle of the portable room, kids hanging from railings and running wildly around me, I remember feeling hopeless and alone. My co-workers were all consumed with activities, and even if they'd been free, what would I have told them? No one could understand what was happening to me, or offer me advice or console me that it wasn't something very serious.

And even though I had my family and my friends and my partner looking after me, I was alone. Somewhere no one that I knew had travelled before. I looked around, scared about what was going on inside my clothing, but having nothing to say for it. No way to tell anyone the truth.

And the unravelling continued at speed. Very soon the fevers and the pain became so persistent that I had to be admitted to hospital to find a solution, once and for all. I was very sick by this stage. I had stopped eating, and I could barely walk. The fevers made my body hurt and the pain from the fistulas were only tempered by absolute, lifeless stillness.

Though I didn't know it, the moment that I had feared was about to unfold: the moment that I had spent the three years since my diagnosis believing would be the end of my world. While I sat in hospital, a nurse who I had never seen before came to see me. She said she was there to introduce me to hospital-grade salt baths, which seemed a reasonable possibility. But I soon discovered it was a way of introducing herself to me, because she was about to become significant in the rest of this experience where my body stopped being known to me simply. The fistulas would not heal, so I would need an ileostomy bag.

In an ileostomy operation, a part of your small bowel called the ileum is brought to the surface of your abdomen to form a stoma. A bag is literally stuck to the skin to ensure the waste from the stoma is collected, essentially bypassing the rest of the digestive system, and giving it time to rest and, hopefully, heal. In my case, even after the ileostomy I would need more surgeries to repair the damage cause by the fistulas, but the doctors believed these patch-ups would have a far better chance of working if the whole area was out of action.

When doctors first tell you about something like this, they tend to let the information out in bits and pieces. In my case, a doctor came to my bed and let me know they were in a bit of a spot, unsure of how to fix the problem. He mentioned the ileostomy bag as a potential solution, but said not to worry about it yet, because it would only be a last resort.

This was the way a parent might break bad news to a child: never straight, and with enough detail missing that you could be forgiven for believing that you were headed for a very different outcome. In the following days, a nurse with orange hair and bright-red lips began circling me, like prey. Coaxing. 'If the ileostomy bag happened, you'd probably only have it for a couple of weeks. A couple of months, tops,' she cooed. The idea was difficult to swallow – but a couple of weeks or a month ... maybe I could manage? Even that turned out not to be true.

I was being primed for what they were already planning to do, the information delivered in a way that was supposed to help me digest it. To come to a point of acceptance. But I was cold with fear. I had been afraid of this moment my whole life. Perhaps this was the shapeless bad thing I had been waiting for since I was a child, the thing sent to test me or to punish me for not praying hard enough.

What had I done to deserve this? How was it possible? How could I even imagine my body in this new and unfamiliar form? It didn't make sense. And its incongruity made me feel ill. I wanted to vomit at the thought.

I lay awake all that night in that hospital room. Surely, this sort of thing didn't actually happen to twenty-something women with their whole lives ahead of them? What a horrible outcome. A terrible end to an already traumatic experience. What would my body look like with an ileostomy bag attached? How could I possibly hide it underneath my clothes? Would everyone know I had one and would they be repulsed by me? How much would it hurt?

This failure of my body to fix itself hurt. It produced a grief that became difficult to bear or to understand, so I shut it out. I talked it down, like it was a complaining child. And like many women, I diminished it as a passing hysteria. But it was wound deep inside the fabric of my body, moving with my blood and causing my limbs to feel heavy.

The hospital room was suffocating. I felt like I had been captured, and there was an inevitability to what was coming.

As much as I forced thoughts of my broken body aside, they would sometimes catch me off guard, causing me to jump. I was constantly trying to maintain perspective, aware that other people had it worse than I did. Sure an ileostomy bag would be tough, but I was lucky that it was even an option. Sure I was ill, but I had the support of free health care. Sure I was alone in my pain, but I had a partner, friends and family who wanted to understand and help me. Sure I couldn't work, but if it all crashed down I would have somewhere to go. But grief is very different from self-pity. Grief is necessary if we want to process a loss. It is a period of mourning that should be honoured. Because if we don't grieve these losses and these changed states, they get stuck inside us, and we fail to understand them properly. We can fail to love them.

The grief wasn't simply about what was happening to me; it was also about the enormity of the task ahead, a grappling with the unknown realm that this twist had placed before me. Coming back to health after operations was tough. I didn't know if I had what it would take to fight my way back.

But as much as I thrashed around inside, when the doctors finally told me that they had met and decided that an ileostomy bag was the only way forward, I smiled nicely and agreed.

***

On the night before the operation, I struggled to keep down the preparation medication, a drink so horrid that I would gag every time I took a sip. I hadn't eaten properly for weeks, so my body was hostile. As the drink made its way through my body, it would jerk and resist and try to come back up. I was too sick to make it to the bathroom most of the time, so I constantly had to call on the nurses, who were surely tiring of my bodily functions being let loose everywhere. I can almost laugh now at the horrible experiences the poor nurses had to endure with me, but I relied on them like my own arms and legs. Nurses sat with me in the midst of disaster again and again, and somehow always treated it as a normal part of their day. The generosity with which they can make you feel like this is just 'what they do' is a positive side of that gap between medical workers and patients, and it still brings me undone.

I felt sick, not only from the medicine, but also at the thought of what was about to happen to me. There was no way out. The night before the operation, my close friends and family came and spent some time with me. They stood around the bed and talked about anything they could think would keep my mind off what was about to happen. The footy, the weather, funny stories about friends and other family. It was as though we were having a dinner party and AJ was the host. He kept everyone entertained while I just lay there. I would hide my face whenever

I began to cry. I didn't want any sympathy. I didn't want anything.

As I was wheeled into the theatre the following day, I was hit by the cold. Theatre is always cold. I hoped they would quickly give me something to ease my panic. When the surgeon came in and described the operation to me, it didn't seem real. It suddenly seemed like such a ridiculous solution to the problem. But I was polite and smiled weakly. I wanted to be gone for longer than the operation time. I wanted them to turn me off for weeks, so all of this would happen without me needing to be there. I knew on the other side I would be changed. And I knew what it would feel like when I woke up and tried to pull myself out of The Nothingness. It would hurt. It would be hard. And I wasn't sure how much energy I would have left to recover.

I reached down to where my belly would soon be supporting a part of my bowel, thrust outside into the world. The place where a bag would be fixed. I kept my hand there as long as I could. I felt around, trying to memorise exactly what it was like. I had never taken much notice of this part of my body before. My fingers felt around slowly. My stomach was flat, almost concave with the lack of food. I was sure I could feel the very slight beat of my heart.

They asked me to count, and I resigned myself to the grief that had welled so high that tears rolled down my cheeks. It felt like a very serious ending to a very serious affair. I believed it was the ending of the life I'd known so far, and that I would wake up to a new one.

As I closed my eyes, I saw the darkened figures of operating staff fade to black, and I travelled to that half-place between living and dying. It's a space of pure absence, The Nothingness. But it's a nothingness that is bookended by fear. On one side, before I went under, that fear was always blanketed by hope. On the other side, when I woke up, for a few precious moments I'd feel relieved that I had made it back. But just as quickly, I'd feel a rush of panic as I gathered myself and quickly assessed the damages. *Who* made it here? How much of me had been altered? Would I recover? What did they find?

I thought they should probably tell you about the fear when you first get diagnosed: 'You will lose feeling in your arms intermittently, and we should also mention that you will frequently wake up in the middle of the night – not always screaming, but definitely scared.' Fear is a shapeshifter. It can manifest as anger, silence, panic, agitation ... the list goes on. But it is threaded right through the experience of being sick.

I entered The Nothingness.

***

I woke to such an enormous rush of pain that it took my breath away. I was in the post-operative bay, my most hated place in the hospital. When I first started going under a general anaesthetic a lot, I would wake up seriously agitated. I think I was agitated because I was confused, because I hated the feeling of being arrested in a holding bay after an operation. I hated the smells of hygiene and the sounds of machines that monitored my status, beeping their cold expertise throughout the room.

I would hear the post-op nurses as they went about their shifts, and their chatter confirmed that the banality of the everyday was alive and well. They would begin conversations at desks and continue them as they went between beds, taking blood pressure and noting heart rates. How could I be in such a different emotional reality to the person who was standing right in front of me? How could my world be turning upside down while someone talked to her colleague about how to win the lotto?

There was no way I could move, and I didn't really want to. I felt so beaten by this enforced physical metamorphosis that I could have easily melted away into nothingness forever.

And I was filled with an immovable anger.

I had always made an effort to treat the hospital staff with kindness, but waking up after the ileostomy operation, I felt that I had been betrayed by all of them. Not one of them had run into the operating theatre and demanded the surgeons take their hands off me. No one had fought for an alternative ending to this story. All I saw in their faces was a smugness that they weren't the ones with a bag attached to their guts. 'Oh you poor thing, it must hurt,' they would say, as if they could ever really know exactly how much pain I was in.

And being wheeled back into my room where my family waited for me, with their desperate looks of hopelessness, only enraged me further. I wanted to be left alone to rage. To scream at cleaners, to throw a glass at the window and tell the night nurses to fuck off. But I didn't; I just allowed the tears to stream down my face as I kept hitting the button that pumped morphine into my body. I didn't want to hear anything from anyone. No one would have anything to say to me that could make it better.

I couldn't move. I was in more pain than I had been in for some time, and while I couldn't see exactly what had happened, I could feel something was wrong, just to the right of my belly button. I can remember the nurses tending to me in the days following the operation, pulling off bandages and changing the bags and telling me what my future might be like. It was done. There was no going back. And I trembled with the sickness of regret. I wished with all of me that I could travel back in time and change things. Not be so complacent. Tell the doctors to look again, because something was wrong.

We have our bodies built into our minds; they are not merely flesh. This change hurt the dreams I'd had for myself. This change in my body meant that I wouldn't be living the life I had imagined. And it broke my heart. The girl that I had loved was gone.

ten

the face of death

My disease had careered out of control. It was in this darkness, where I had lost the line that I had been tracing, that I realised that anything was possible. No longer was there a reliable storyline with a beginning, a middle and a safe, happy end. Instead, the road could take me anywhere, like in the *Choose Your Own Adventure* books that I'd read as a child: one wrong page-turn, and you've walked straight into the lava pit. And it was here, in this realisation, that I became truly aware of the possibility that I could die.

When you're very ill, it is not easy to explain this fear of death to the people around you – how you feel it more now. It's like that bright flash in the sky that no one else was there to see. Why didn't I talk about it? For one, I knew that most of the time the people I talked to would try to explain that fear away as nonsense, or at least no more than a passing concern. I'd be told that fear was irrational, the result of an overactive mind; that it was brought on by mild hysteria, or by reading the wrong websites, or not keeping perspective. 'Don't worry, you're going to be okay.' But at the heart of the silence about fear was the hopelessness of trying to be rid of it. The only thing that would rid me of fear, would be getting rid of the disease.

Chronic illness is like being thrown an existential curve ball that leaves you grabbing at the air. When your body's not safe, the equation concludes, you are not safe. And so even if an illness isn't likely to be fatal, it still provides a fertile ground for the awareness of death to flourish. In its very pure state, fear as it relates to illness is a normal reaction to a real danger. But when it finds its way into every part of your life, it becomes a problem in itself.

Fear is much more than a wrong step along the emotional tundra. It is the shudder down your spine when you realise that all the things you had been bothered by, the tiny little things that had obsessed you — your work, the neighbour's noisy dog, the lady at the cake shop who was rude, whether your hair flicked in the right direction — were all the concerns of someone who had no idea. Someone who believed that they were going to live forever. Fear is that moment that you wake up, breathless, grabbing at your throat and gasping for air because it's just dawned on you that you were tricked into believing that things were going to work out.

Fear changes the way your eyes focus, so that the world seems to move subtly faster or slower, leaving you ever so slightly out of step. You are looking in at ordinary life from behind the window, and that feeling is utterly frightening, because who are we when all of the regular humdrum of our lives is stripped away?

I began to wonder whether fear was more of a knowledge, knowledge that we are human and going to die. Even the small scares we all experience now and then, when you think something might be worse than it is, or when you find out that things are worse than you'd realised, illuminate the faith with which we generally live our lives. Somehow, while we know that we may be struck down with illness or death at any time, it always comes as a shock. We simply don't believe it will happen to us. How else could it shake us the way it does?

My sister-in-law Bec is a beautiful, healthy human brimming with the energy of an adventurer. After leaving her home in the UK to travel the world, she met my brother and moved to Australia. Now in her mid-thirties, her energy is still intoxicating.

One morning, when she was playing basketball outside with her seven-year-old child, her heart shuddered and skipped a beat. Her left arm shot with pain and she immediately felt sick. After second-guessing herself numerous times, she called an ambulance. 'They weren't sure whether they'd bother [taking me to hospital], I'm not a candidate for a heart attack.' But they decided to take her as a precaution, and on the way to the hospital she had a heart attack. Later that day she was diagnosed with spontaneous coronary artery dissection (SCAD), a rare form of heart disease that strikes young, healthy women and is often missed in diagnosis because heart disease is rarely experienced by this cohort.

I remember seeing her days after her diagnosis; her face was ashen and filled with the quiet panic that comes in the wake of this kind of sudden experience. It's a panic that has your eyes darting, like at any moment you will be set upon by some hidden predator. You are only slightly aware of what is going on around you, because you feel like suddenly it's the silence, the gaps between the walls, the spaces around you that could harbour danger – all the unexpected places.

Even after receiving a diagnosis of SCAD, she was left confused about what this would actually 'mean'. And each time it was explained to her, by a different specialist with a different history of experience with SCAD, it was given a slightly different spin. No one's answers were exactly the same. What were the signs that she needed to look out for if this kind of attack was to be avoided in the future? What were the frightening fluttering feelings that she was still experiencing? What did it mean that she was still feeling a heaviness in her arms and a change of beat in her heart? Because there were no clear answers to any of her questions, there was no clear direction for her to manage this ongoing disease, and no sense of how it might affect her life. Could she die?

The possibility of death, of course, is always part of the deal. Somehow we busy ourselves so thoroughly that we are able to convince ourselves that we can avoid it, but illness means that you can't be busy anymore, and death comes keenly into focus.

Thanatophobia, or 'death anxiety' is a condition characterised by a fear of one's own mortality. Humans have always contemplated their death. Throughout history and in many parts of the world, people have believed that death is inflicted by deities, and that certain illnesses are the manifestation of evil and a sign of unknown doom to follow. It's the unknown that frightens us, the unknown of when and how we will die. As the great philosopher Dumbledore said in *Harry Potter and the Half-Blood Prince*, 'It is the unknown we fear when we look upon death and darkness, nothing more.'

Ironically, for the chronically ill, death is sometimes the only thing that seems certain, though to reckon with your own death is another step altogether.

***

Each time I was admitted to hospital, I would pray for a room to myself, but usually I would find myself sharing with a ragtag bunch of people who I probably wouldn't have crossed paths with normally.

On this particular hospital admission, I was sharing my room with three others, our beds divided only by thin curtains that were sometimes pulled open to reveal us to the room. In these situations, I would get to know my roommates in a way that even people who had known them for years might not. Depending on how bedridden I was, and how often those thin curtains were pulled closed, I could rely on what I overheard to get a picture of who I was sharing with. I would spend hours imagining what they might look like or what might have brought them there.

I would lie still to maximise the opportunity to overhear words or phrases that might slowly fill in gaps. If AJ was in the room with me, I would wave at him to be quiet whenever I thought I might be missing something crucial in the next cubicle. Did they say pancreas? Or weight loss?

I was aware that this was probably being done in reverse, so I would always order my visitors to speak quietly – I didn't want to make it too easy for the rest of the room; there was no pride in getting the information via a loud-mouthed family member.

It often took a considerable amount of time to put all the pieces together, but after a couple of days I could draw a fairly comprehensive picture of my fellow inmates. Married? Yes. Kids? Only two, and one hadn't visited yet. Which nurse do they hate? Stephanie on night shift. She never answers her buzzer and is curt. She also scratched his arm when she was changing his sheet. He thinks she meant to.

But more than that, I got to know them on an intimate level that only a hospital room could allow. What happens on ward seven stays on ward seven, so to speak. We are laid bare in hospital rooms, and fears that we usually hold deep down are unleashed. At times I could hear the very moment someone broke, as they called out to the nurses in the middle of the night. If the cries sounded urgent, I would stiffen in bed. I could hear how scared they were. If the nurses attended and turned on more than the night lights, I knew it was serious. As a very last resort, doctors would be called to work out whether the patient should be taken to theatre or given a stronger shot of something. At the very worst, they were wheeled out and didn't return, and I would never find out what happened to them.

A hospital runs around the clock: there is no such thing, really, as day and night. Even as the sun rose and fell in the sky, the world inside the hospital didn't feel very different. Sickness doesn't take any notice of the sun. Instead, for me, time was experienced as an energy that moved through the rooms. I could gauge what time it was by the level of fear in the air, the calls for help becoming more urgent as night fell. At night, fear had endless potential and exponential growth, which, thankfully, struggled to survive during the day. Bells would ring insistently through the corridors, calling for nurses to attend one situation after another. I'd hear them moving around, talking about which patients were annoying them. It always seemed the night might never end.

***

I encountered death many times in hospital, but one particular experience stuck with me. I had been in hospital for a couple of days. My roommates were a motley crew, but the one I remember the most was a much older man whose bed was adjacent to mine. I remember the heaviness of his breathing, and the way it sounded like my grandad's before he died.

He was visited every day by his wife, who had obviously done this many times before. She had the drill down perfectly: pick up a magazine and coffee from the cafe on the way up, then something sweet from the vending machine at 11am. She'd make a couple of calls and let people know how he was doing, but most of the time they would just sit together in silence. I wondered if that was how marriages went after a long time, drifting into a silence that was comforting and soft and often only ruptured by the occasional small laugh, shared while watching something on television.

He stuck in my mind, because to me he was simply old and sick and was probably going to die. I had that sense of sadness that you feel for someone you don't really know, where you feel kind-of sorry for them because, of course, dying is hard, but there's a distance. It was impossible for me to reach over to where they sat, only metres away, and understand what it felt like. I was in my early twenties; I guessed that they must have been in their late seventies. For me, it fit into that neat storyline we all understand: you get old, and then you die. This storyline was so far from my own that it barely registered. There was nothing particularly alarming about it.

That was, until everything changed.

A nurse came to take my routine, very regular, very mundane vitals. Blood pressure, heart rate and temperature. If there is one measurement of time that you can rely on in hospital, it's the regularity with which your vitals will be checked. On this occasion, something was wrong. My heart rate had dropped to below 30 beats per minute, and the machine was making alarming noises. A doctor was called to double-check what the nurse had seen.

Before I knew what was happening, an announcement came over the speakers: 'Code blue'. Code blue? I'd heard this announcement many times before, but this time code blue was being directed to my floor and to my bed. My mind began racing. I looked at the doctor as he decided whether to use a defibrillator – whether my heart needed to be shocked back into action. Suddenly, the room was filled with fifteen doctors who had come from every part of the hospital.

I lay there, a stunned rabbit in front of an expectant group of hunters. I was frozen in the gaping face of the unknown. Everything that I had understood about living told me I was in danger. My mind was empty but my body rushed with an urgent response. *I might be dying,* it whispered, *this might be it.*

I can't really tell you what happened next, except that, by itself, my heart rate returned to a less concerning pace. I suspect the simple shock of having fifteen doctors suddenly appear in my room may have had something to do with it. As the emergency staff all made their way back to whatever they had been doing before, the doctor who had raised the alarm mumbled something about being safe rather than sorry, and everything returned to normal. Like nothing had happened.

But the event had profoundly affected me. In that instant, when the code blue had been called, I'd realised that the elderly guy in the next bed and I were the same. I could just as easily have been lying in his bed with his wife by my side, and he could have been over here in mine. I was just as fragile and mortal and capable of dying as he was. The only difference between us, up to that point, had been that he was probably already reckoning with it. He may have had sleepless nights after feeling a small twinge on his left side, and wondered if it was about to be his time. That time may have already come for a few of his friends, so he would have had some warning that it was possible. And I had not. Of course I'd known I could die, but not really, not really, *really* die.

There had been so many moments that could have alerted me to the fact that death is always with us, but I'd foolishly waved them away and believed what I always had: that death happened to other people. I'd comfort myself with the fact that Crohn's disease is not itself fatal. Though I knew it could have life-threatening developments, I'd never considered that this might happen to me. Even knowing all the things that could go wrong every time I was put under general anaesthetic, every time I went under the knife, hadn't been enough to make it sink in.

We are always looking for reasons to explain why someone has died, reasons that make them different to us. We need to understand why a death has occurred, because logic and reason can negate the more frightening possibility that it is all just chance. 'She shouldn't have been out at night', 'He drank too much', 'They were old', 'They were driving too fast'. We need to believe that there is nothing random about it.

Our brains do their best to keep us from dwelling on our inevitable demise. A study at Bar Ilan University in Israel found that the brain shields us from existential fear by categorising death as an unfortunate event that only befalls other people. 'The brain does not accept that death is related to us,' said the study's lead author, Dr Yair Dor-Ziderman. 'We have this primal mechanism that means when the brain gets information that links self to death, something tells us it's not reliable, so we shouldn't believe it.' Being shielded from thoughts of our future death could be crucial for us to live in the present.

That moment when the lights were flashing on my heart monitor and the doctors stood before me (I'll admit in my memory most of them looked quite bored) was shocking. The realisation hit me with such blinding clarity that I knew I could never go back. In the initial moments following this sort of awakening, you are usually hit with a surge of adrenalin that keeps you up all night, rolling around with the concept of death for days on end.

In every sickness story, death is the sullen teenager on a family holiday, sitting in the back of the car with headphones in, spoiling any sense of joy or adventure. I'd wonder if this figure of death was behind all the tricks my illness played. Who else would find this game so enjoyable, insisting that it go on and on?

***

Following the ileostomy, I was gentle with every movement, scared that something I might do would break me. I was scared of going anywhere near the site for fear I would touch something that I didn't want to touch. I kept my eyes up as much as possible and turned away when I was asked to look at it. I wasn't ready.

But just as I was recovering, the world twisted again. I remember a lurching pain and not being able to keep anything down. Nothing, not even a drop of water would stay in my body. I couldn't stop throwing up. The nurses came in and out, and tried to work out how to stop it. I had scrunched the bedsheets up into my hands. Holding on. I had now seen how things could go wrong; I now knew that it wasn't unlikely that something bad would happen.

Soon enough, they assessed that my bowel was obstructed.

I remember one nurse, a rotund man who seemed to have way too much empathy for a long career in this job. To stop the vomiting, he had to insert a nasogastric tube through my nose all the way down into my stomach. He told me with fake cheer that, though he'd been a nurse for many years, he hadn't done much of this sort of thing for a while. But I wasn't to worry because they would keep trying until they got it right.

So many experiences in hospital involve health staff who haven't performed a procedure for a long time, or very often – or, the most frightening, it's the first time they've ever done it. It's part of the exchange, though, and often you take on the role of a supportive parent, coaxing them through and letting them know that you think they're doing a good job: *Don't take any notice of my face, I overreact.* Once, when a junior nurse spilled my blood all over a once-clean floor trying to get a bung in my arm, I told her it was fine: 'This sort of thing happens all the time.' Quietly though, I was praying that the three-strike rule was in effect. In hospitals, the three-strike rule maintains that if you don't get a procedure right in the first three attempts, you need to find someone who is a little further up the chain to take over the process.

The nurse inserting the tube into my nose was experienced, he just hadn't done this particular procedure in a while. Still, the fear had been put into me.

Resisting the desire to gag and instead trying to swallow the tube and allow it to pass through to my stomach was beyond hard – it was excruciating. But so too was the pain of the obstructed bowel. I could barely speak. I lay there in a drugged stupor trying to pull apart the various sources of pain so that I could deal with them, separated and weakened. But it was overwhelming, and it took every bit of energy that I had just to keep existing. It felt at times like I drifted off, but it wasn't into sleep. I must have gone in and out of consciousness, because for brief periods I escaped my body and the pain stopped. But for the most part, I was lodged securely within an increasingly unbearable pain.

***

When my family and friends came to visit, their reactions made it clear that I was quite a sight. AJ would be there around the clock and the nurses would let him stay after closing hours. They stood around the bed just watching me, speaking quietly to each other. I still couldn't really speak, so instead, over the next couple of days, they took turns holding my hand. The memory of this utterly simple act has risen above most others from that time, because it tilted the game just enough for me to begin to see it anew. The holding of hands is such a human thing. When it all comes down to it, it is probably one of the great symbols of love. Its power made sense to me in a way it never had before.

A few years before, when my Grandad Reggie was in the final stages of dying, members of my family had all taken it in turns to hold his hand. We were pretty much on shifts: as one person let go, he would be ready to grab the next hand. Even when he was teetering in and out of life, his grasp was strong. He couldn't tell us, but it felt at the time like what he was holding onto was this important connection to his life. He was holding onto me, a grandchild, and to my mum, his daughter, and to all his children and grandchildren. He could touch through the generations and the lives that had also been his. And we were holding onto him in the same way – reaching back to where his life touched the ones that had gone before him.

Grandad Reggie had loomed large in our family. He had grown up on a farm at Purnim, a small town near Warrnambool in Western Victoria. As a young man, he moved with his wife and young family to Melbourne and worked in a milk processing dairy until he retired. By the time I met him, he was a funny, gentle man, who spent his days in a huge shed out the back of his old house, or in his garden. He would fry mashed potatoes for us as we sat around his dining table for big Sunday-night family dinners, and we would wander around his garden and into his hothouse before dinner was served. When we finally left, almost time for bed, he would hand each of us a brown paper bag of boiled lollies with our name on it.

Through holding his hands in those last days I was taken to his garden, where he'd taught me how to run fast so I could beat the boys in my class. He'd point to my knees and tell me to lift them up high and keep my back straight: 'You lift them up and God will put them down.' He'd had a promising sprinting career, until he broke down after qualifying for the Stawell Gift.

In the years before his death, Grandad Reggie and Nana Les relocated next door to my parents. I would drive to their house now and then to help them with shopping or cleaning, or just to keep them company. One day, I found him just after he'd had an accident, sitting at the end of his bed in wet pants. I helped him into new trousers and then sat on the bed beside him, on top of a doona cover we'd given them years ago to celebrate their fifty years of marriage.

I was a grandchild of his and keenly aware how strange it must have been for him to need my help in such an intimate way. The accident had rattled him. I could tell he was agitated by this increasingly frequent loss of control. He held my elbow and looked at me sheepishly, whispering close to me, in a way that made me think he was about to reveal a great family secret: 'Am I going to be alright?'

I was taken aback by the absurdity of the question. He was dying. We didn't know how, or have precise clarity around what was wrong with him, because testing had proven difficult. But his body had begun to break down and his death was coming. None of us thought about it like that, because death wasn't something we ever directly thought about, but it was an unacknowledged fact.

As I sat silent, Reggie turned away, clearly unsure if he should have asked me, or whether he even wanted an answer. I didn't quite know what to do, and so I did the only thing I could bear to do. I tried to find his eyes but chickened out. 'Yes, yes, you're absolutely going to be alright. I promise you,' I lied.

I've thought about this moment so many times since. Should I have faced it with him? Should we have tried to reckon with what was really about to happen? I regret that we didn't. I regret the loss of that moment, when I could have said the things that never get said. Instead, we pretended nothing was happening. Of course, he knew that I was lying, but at that moment it suited us both to continue on with the game.

In the days following my ileostomy, I felt just like my Grandad Reggie when he faced his death: like someone watching a storm rolling over the hills in the distance, making quick calculations as to when it will hit. Reggie didn't have the same protection as his wife, who had dementia and was blissfully unaware of her fragility. He died much earlier than she did, and it left me wondering if you can know death into existence. I now knew how it must have felt for him to face the uncertainty alone.

There is something uniquely powerful about holding hands. As I lay there with my hand being held by family and friends, I could understand what an important link this gesture was to the world that I loved. In that moment, when pain reduced me to my simple atomic structure, I could feel Reggie. I felt like he was me and I was him. I felt like babies must feel before they see themselves in the mirror, when they are everyone and everyone is them. I knew for sure what it must have felt like for Reggie to receive that love through each hand that held his. And I realised that the process of dying is expressed and experienced through the people who bear witness to it.

One of my friends, Ineke, was there holding my hand that day. We've been friends for thirty years now, and it feels like she knows something about me that I could never explain to anyone else. She held me and saw me at my most broken, and I have never had to explain myself to her since then. I feel like, silently, I told her all of it that day.

It means a lot for someone to hold your hand through the process of illness — something that, like death, cannot be changed, or stopped. When I've spoken to AJ about this time, it's clear how difficult it was for him to bear witness, watching as I lost so much weight and drifted in and out of a drugged haze. Each night, he would struggle out of the hospital and find himself home alone, broken by this tsunami that had crashed around us. Neither of us had any choice but to find our own way to acceptance. This couldn't be stopped.

For me, the key was to surrender. I was the most fragile and vulnerable I had ever been, with no fight left in me to combat this disease and its constant surprises. I no longer felt sure of what it could or couldn't do to me. I realised that I had to allow whatever was going to happen, to happen. And it was a choice, to stop trying to hold back the floodwaters.

***

Those couple of days, and a particularly long and lonely night, set me on a completely different course when it came to my understanding of death and, as an extension, how I could live with illness. Until then, I had been afraid of death and was unable to remove it from all the mythology and fiction that I had grown up with. But I now understood that living and dying are always right there beside each other. To live well you must know death, but to die well you must know life.

As with the topic of illness, most people don't really want to talk about death, but I couldn't speak or think of anything else for some time. I craved conversation with someone who could understand what I'd been through and help me find words to explain it. But this kind of conversation rarely went the way I wanted because, firstly, I probably seemed *way* too keen to speak about death, and, secondly, for some people the whole topic can feel depressing or negative, or so inconclusive that they decide there's no point talking about it. It is also a troubling reminder to others of your state of health.

In my case, I learned to listen out for hints dropped in casual conversation that would expose the kind of person who had contemplated their own mortality. Prodding usually revealed that this had come about because they had seen people they loved grapple with death or had themselves felt close to it at some point.

It was hard to have seen behind the curtain at a time when no one else my age had even thought to look. So I set about my own private mission to get to the bottom of it. To understand death so that I could go on without it sulking in the back seat of my car. I began with *The Tibetan Book of Living and Dying* and moved slowly through all the mystics. Even some of the cheesier Western thinkers had some space on my bookshelf. I also watched endless episodes of a series called *I Survived, Beyond and Back* about near-death experiences. In the years before, I'd often found myself gasping for air in the middle of the night, having dreamed about the nothingness that I feared waited for me after I died. But I replaced those fears with something I could hold onto, an amalgam of all these theories on death.

Dealing with death was the first step towards realising that I needed to drastically shift how I understood and dealt with the world, and my place within it.

eleven

aboard a sinking ship

It took days and days, but slowly I built enough strength to get out of bed, with some help, and made it to the bathroom to assess the results of the operation. When I looked in the mirror and saw my body, I didn't know it any more. I wanted to vomit. It frightened me.

It wasn't the body I had grown up inside. It had scars that ran across its middle and a bag that hung on it like a mistake. Over the following weeks of recovery, I tried to avoid looking at it. I moved as quickly as I could past any mirrors and avoided lifting my head in the bathroom. I wished that mirrors didn't exist. Before, there'd been some talk of me only needing the ileostomy for a few months, but after the operation all such talk disappeared. The doctors never spoke to me again about timelines or about how difficult it might be to reverse the operation – if it was even possible. I would simply have to adjust.

One day, a nurse approached my bed with a pair of scissors in her hand. For some reason, I remember those scissors. It was one of the first moments AJ and I were alone after the operation. For weeks, there had been a constant stream of family and friends in and out of my room. I had come through some tricky nights, but it finally felt as if the world was settling. I had spoken to this nurse before – she was a specialist ileostomy nurse – and I will never forget her sharp haircut and bright-red lipstick.

As with all medical staff, when she walked in, I tried to sit up and look cheerful. I wanted her to treat me well. She placed the scissors onto a trolley stationed at the end of my bed and started riffling through the different gauzes, trying to find the right one to stick to my body. While she was searching, she began making what I thought was friendly small talk.

'Most relationships don't last,' she said casually. 'Not after these sorts of operations.'

She barely looked up. If she had, she would have seen a couple of kids in their twenties shattered by what they had just been through. She would have seen me, utterly shamed by my new body. Not knowing how to use it. Wiped out by all the drugs. And AJ, trying to look like he knew what was going on, though in truth he was overwhelmed by uncertainty about what his new life with me might involve. In my version of this memory, she is smiling when she says this. I can't be sure, but I remember thinking she was enjoying how vulnerable we both were, lost together in a sea of trauma.

'Pardon?' I smiled, clenching my fists and hoping that I had misheard.

She grinned, feigning sympathy. 'It's just, I've seen this before. It's tough to maintain a relationship after an operation like this. People break up. I thought you should both know.'

I felt sick. I was trapped, unable to get away from her. I didn't need to ask her what she meant. It was clear that she wanted to be the one to tell me I was no longer attractive or useful. I felt like an idiot. Of course relationships didn't last through 'this sort of thing'. Why would they? She had hit me directly where I was most vulnerable, and she got to me so easily because I was ashamed. I was ashamed of my body. Ashamed of what it couldn't do naturally anymore. I was ashamed that I was going to need help just to get through each day.

While I'd been in hospital, we'd had to accept that I wouldn't be able to go back to our house in Carlton North, where I had spent so many days in my turret. I hadn't realised, when I rushed to hospital weeks before, that I would never return, but it had become clear that I wouldn't be able to look after myself for several months, or work enough for us to pay the rent. So while I was recovering in hospital, AJ was packing up our home. The ceiling-high bookshelves in the study, the kitchen that was so tiny it could only fit two of us, the poky staircase that led to our bedroom: I would have to commit it all to memory, because I wasn't going to see it again.

I felt as though my life was being taken apart piece by piece. Every tiny object that I had gathered, like a bowerbird might gather shiny things, was either being thrown away or packed into a storage box. The things being thrown away probably didn't look like much, but each pen or piece of paper or ripped T-shirt was a sentence in a larger story. Each piece of junk, and how it had been arranged in my house, reflected my life back to me. It was stupid, I knew it, but lying in that hospital room looking out across the rooftops of Fitzroy, I felt like I was the one being disassembled. Taken apart, bit by bit until I had nothing to show for my life.

What made it harder was that this was being done in the name of love. My family and friends were trying to keep my life together, hoping that after the operation, a few adjustments, and a small detour here and there, this illness wouldn't amount to more than a small bump in the road. One day I'd be able to look back and laugh about that time when everything in my life went backwards.

But I was lost. That small physical change had sent me into a spin. I didn't know where my centre was anymore. What I had lost was a deep part of myself, the part that belonged only to me.

The long and short of it was that AJ and I would have to live in my childhood home. Without a doubt, I was one of the lucky ones: I had a family who owned a home and who could take me in if and when I needed. So many others in my situation have nowhere to go. Still, it would be the first time in just under a decade that I lived there, and the idea filled me with panic.

***

On the day I was discharged, my parents picked me up in their old HJ Holden. It was wholly familiar: vinyl seats with rips covered in gaffer tape, and the tape deck playing my father's easy-listening hits on panpipe and the latest from Acker Bilk. Sitting in that back seat spun me violently into the past. It was like my life had been totally erased, as if nothing I had done in the past decade mattered at all.

I had always found it strange returning home after an admission. There aren't many circumstances where a stay in hospital won't change you. Usually I had seen things I'd thought

I wouldn't see for decades to come, and sometimes, after an operation, I had fresh hope that life might return to normal. So coming home was almost like returning from a long trip overseas, and it was mostly too hard to explain the profound experience to anyone who wasn't there – it took some time to get used to being back.

But this was a whole new level. This particular stay had only been a fortnight or so, but I didn't feel like I fit the world anymore. After such a long time of hating the very idea of hospital, I wanted to stay. I was getting a glimpse of what it must feel like to be institutionalised. The routines. The days punctuated by the regularity of treatment. The food. The smells. The light. The night nurses. How my skin smelled after certain drugs. The hours spent preparing for something I knew would be painful, and then the relief when it was done. Despite my fear, something had clicked, and I realised I now felt more at home there than anywhere. Because above all things, a hospital promises to keep you alive.

As I sat in the Holden, my distress was obvious. On top of that, my internal narrative was mocking that distress, loudly putting me back in my place. Who the hell did I think I was anyway? I was like an angry child who'd finally made a run for the road, only to find that I didn't actually know how to cross it. My internal adult sharply pulled me back from the kerb with a shake of her head. *What did you think you were doing?*

***

As I walked through the front doors of my family home, I got a rush of dread and panic. The TV was on in the lounge room and the gas heater was glowing with the heat that was pumped out of it from morning till night right through winter. My running trophies had been taken down from a shelf in the kitchen, but a medal still hung there, as a reminder of what I once was. The scene was familiar, but I returned to it now different. It confused me.

My mum and dad rushed around trying to make me feel comfortable. It was a relief to have them cook my food and wash my clothes. I could tell by the way that they both looked at me that they would do anything to help me, that they would swap places with me if they could. But I was hardened, and it was difficult to accept any kindness the way I knew I should.

I didn't trust my body. I didn't know who I was anymore, and I was back in a space that was so familiar and yet now so foreign. AJ carried our bags to my old bedroom, where we planned to rest until we were strong enough to move on.

My breathing quickened as the fluoro lights in the kitchen disoriented me. I realised I didn't know where to find any comfort. There was nothing that I could imagine that would bring me relief from the searing pain in my body, and the overwhelming panic that I was lost. I didn't belong here anymore, but there was nowhere else to go.

In those first few hours, I was like an animal being hunted: hyper-alert to any strange flicker of movement in my body. I was convinced that my bowel would become obstructed again, so I lay quietly on my bed, waiting for something to go wrong. I lay like this for weeks, really.

I had travelled back in time, back to the place where my identity had been formed. It was great, and it was warm, but I felt like a teenager being forced to participate. A family's day-to-day life is a type of barn dance – one with enormous room for error, but nonetheless a vital interdependent set of steps that needed to be followed. My older brother had moved out long before, but my younger brother and sister had returned home while they finished their degrees. My parents had bought the house soon after they were married and my dad had eventually built on additions that meant the house was now long enough to hide in, if you needed to. I went to my old bedroom and put my head into my pillow. I put on some old Patti Smith and sunk beneath the utter comfort of her power in the opening lyrics of 'Gloria'. I hoped I might be able to continue to sink and hide forever.

When you surrender your ability to do things for yourself, you are not just giving up your functionality and autonomy, you are then required to engage in a new set of agreements with anyone who has offered to help you. It requires high-level negotiating skills. What I was negotiating was the gravelled path of a new relationship dynamic that, on my side, bounced between gratitude, hostility and guilt that I was anything but grateful for the kindness I was being shown. Because it also felt like I was negotiating away my stake in the game, and it was difficult to let go, to sit idly while my partner and parents made decisions on my behalf.

Our intimate relationships are woven with delicate threads, so intertwined that sometimes they can't be pulled apart. Hours can be spent trying to unpick all the knots and twists in order to rework them into something new. But they are easily broken. You need to understand their fragility, and you certainly can't be complacent.

People change. I've always marvelled at people who can maintain a friendship from childhood well into adulthood. How many versions of you have existed since that time? Since you were the person who thought the Roadrunner and Bart Simpson were the funniest things you'd ever seen? Or the person who hung that poster of U2 on your wall? How many times have your beliefs undergone a thorough examination and prompted an about-face? How many different hairstyles have you had? It takes incredibly resilient relationships to see you through each metamorphosis.

When you get sick, you throw a serious challenge into the mix. It's not only you that changes, but the fine threads that hold your relationships together. In each relationship we play certain roles with each other: we take the lead in some, we ride shotgun in others. We adopt roles that inform the shapes of our relationships: we are parents, we are children, we are first-borns, we are gendered, we are cultured. So when our role is altered, when we become sick, it changes the very structure of those relationships.

Such was my privilege that I didn't realise how much I valued my independence until I lost it. Independence is the power to make decisions when and how you want to. To lose that power to medical staff, to government workers, and even to your own loved ones is a shocking blow.

I was very weak, still very sick and uncomfortable with my new body and in need of a high level of personal care. Everything I did now was dealt with in a kind of bureaucracy, and therefore it was done at a snail's pace. I had to wait to be fed, wait until a nurse arrived to help me shower. I had to hope that someone might drive me down to the shops and help me to get a coffee, then take me home again to help me get into bed.

The power dynamic between me and everyone in my life, from my partner to each friend who dropped by to help out, had shifted. I also felt it with my parents. Parent–child relationships necessarily go through these kinds of shifts, though they usually follow a set course: roles can switch, and it's not uncommon for the power dynamics to reverse. This often causes disruption, for example when a teenager seeks more independence or when a parent needs care at the later stages of their life, their child often takes on a parenting-type role. But it is challenging when an adult child returns to requiring care from the family.

Returning to the dependent role of the child is not as simple as reverting to a former self. There is no way that you can return entirely to where you were before, because of the experiences that you have had since childhood.

So parent and child are stuck performing roles that resemble those of the past but that are fundamentally different because they are being played by fundamentally different people. The familiarity can be confusing.

For me, it wasn't so much the fact that I didn't want to be cared for by my parents, because their care was thoughtful and kind and exactly what I needed; it was more that I knew there would be no progress for me here, there was nothing new to find. It was a holding bay, like the ones I'd been in after every operation, and it gave me a similar feeling of agitation – a desire to move as far as possible from the experience was running through me like a bolt of electricity. But I couldn't move.

I was grateful for the help, but fundamentally I wished I didn't need it. There was a deep resistance to the experience, compounded by how public these interdependent relationships made it. And going through these traumatic experiences with other people means that they are experiencing their own pain and loss and hope and expectations.

It's difficult being a carer for someone with an illness, and that caring doesn't need to be full-time; simply being close to someone who is struggling with their health can cause complex issues. Compassion fatigue is a condition that affects carers and those in intimate relationships with people who have chronic or terminal illnesses. The Compassion Fatigue Awareness Project has detailed this issue in this way: 'Day in, day out, workers struggle to function in caregiving environments that constantly present heart-wrenching, emotional challenges.' It's a state of exhaustion and dysfunction, and can be hugely damaging to a relationship.

But even with all these complexities, those who are alone when they're sick often say they would give anything for the support of people close to them. They would do anything to be caught in the difficult emotional world of what it means to be in receipt of the kindness of friends and family. If you happen to be at an age where your parents are no longer with you, and your children have left home and your marriage has long since resolved into separation, sickness can be an incredibly frightening thing.

This is where Ruth Pitt found herself after a successful career and a busy life as a mother of two. As she described in an article in *The Guardian*, she was comfortably 'successful and single'. Then she was hit by a flare-up of her Crohn's disease and found herself alone in a bathroom in the middle of the night forcing pain relief down her throat in an attempt to get some sleep. What she desired, after many years of being joyfully single, was the relief that is brought when you can lean on someone else to get you through: 'I've spent plenty of time in hospital over the last six months, watching loyal husbands bringing toiletry bags in and taking washing home, dimly aware that I can't take the same for granted.'

***

When you're in your mid-twenties, you generally don't choose a partner based on their capacity to care for you. Most of us just imagine that if it all goes well, about fifty-odd years henceforth one partner will draw the shorter straw and wind up explaining to nursing-home staff how their beloved likes their pasta al dente or needs their steak chopped up into triangles. It's nowhere near front-of-mind that the person you've decided to share this part of your life with may soon become your carer. And not many of us are born with an innate ability to take on such a role. Caring requires such a specialised skill set: to understand how to breathe in unison with another. To be so in step that you can walk *for* them.

AJ had the wind knocked out of him also. His days were now suspended. He had been arrested in flight and was now living with his in-laws in the suburbs, waiting it out to see what might become of us.

AJ and I understood, well before the nurse in the hospital told us, that it was going to be tough to find our way through this illness together. Studies show that marriages in which one spouse has a chronic illness are more likely to fail if the spouses are young, and spouses who are caregivers are six times more likely to be depressed than spouses who are not.

In the article 'Don't let chronic illness weaken the bond between you and your partner', Karen Bruno writes about how partnerships are tested when the balance shifts:

> 'Having a chronic illness such as diabetes, arthritis, or multiple sclerosis can take a toll on even the best relationship. The partner who's sick may not feel the way he or she did before the illness. And the person who's not sick may not know how to handle the changes. The strain may push both people's understanding of "in sickness and in health" to its breaking point.'

What I do know is that illness challenged my young relationship specifically in areas that we hadn't developed. What were our roles? What should we have expected of each other? What would we do when one of us woke the other up at 3am in a cold sweat to say they no longer wanted the life we'd found ourselves in? The early days, maybe even years, of illness were marked with the fear that we were going to get it wrong. We believed we had only a small window to set the right course, but we had no role models to follow – none of our friends had been through any of this. No one else needed to work out who they *really* were at such a young age. And during this time, we made a lot of mistakes.

While we build an identity around illness, it can often collide with other identities that are still being formed. When you're young, you are trying to find out who you are and how you fit into the world, so if you become ill, you must grapple with how illness has changed you before you've even had time to work out what 'you' means. You are more likely to identify with your illness, because it's almost all you've known.

This is also true of relationships that have not yet had a chance to form before illness strikes. AJ and I hadn't had the opportunity to really grow into our relationship before we had to deal with chronic illness. Previously we had both been fiercely independent; our relationship was one between two independent individuals. Perhaps in time we might have grown into co-dependency, but if so, illness dramatically fast-tracked that process.

When illness comes knocking on the door, it can be challenging to find a place for it in your relationship. And when the illness is chronic, with no end in sight, it can be hard to imagine that one person caring indefinitely for the other might be an attractive prospect. Who wants to be in a relationship where you are in constant need, or constantly needed? Even though I was being assured – by AJ and by everyone around me – that my needs were legitimate and my requests for help welcome, it didn't take away the persistent feeling that I was a burden on people who might have preferred their life without me. I had, without consultation, changed how the people around me now had to live.

When I'd first started feeling sick, I'd done everything I could to avoid the reality of what it was doing to me. I tried desperately to keep up with my friends. So important were our nightly rituals – bar crawls, band rooms, late-night dancing – that I wouldn't listen to my body's cries to ease up.

By the time I'd made it through the ileostomy operation, I couldn't understand what anyone would see in me anymore. Who would want to engage in a friendship with me? Not just intimate partnerships, but all relationships. I'd seen so much evidence that I was only as good as what I could bring to the world – at that point, how much fun and carefreeness I could bring — that I felt hopeless. I couldn't imagine what I offered anyone anymore.

I became cross at how exposed I was, and how vulnerable I had become in relationships. I had to begin a long process of rebuilding myself and my world.

***

In the early days, AJ and I used to joke about what we might say at the each other's funerals. We each threatened to use that moment to have the final say and draw a picture of the other one that they would hate. We would tell the grieving crowd, who would be hanging on our every word, about secret passions that no one else knew about: 'He loved to dance, but he was never brave enough to show you the beautiful movements and shapes that he could create. So, he danced in private...' He had a similar story for me: 'She had a quiet obsession with hot-air ballooning, but was too fearful to ever take a flight.' We would laugh and continue to add to the composite, always to each other's horrified delight. It's easy to mock something that's way, way, way off on the horizon. Then I got really sick, and suddenly it didn't feel so much like a joke anymore.

As AJ took on the role of carer and I became the cared-for, the rules in our relationship changed, but there was no director there to take us aside and talk us through the new storyline. We had no idea what our new roles would involve, and so there was a lot of fumbling around, bumping into each other. It was as if our legs were tied together for a three-legged race: if one of us tried to get out ahead of the other, we'd both fall down.

If we'd known at the start that I was going to get so sick I would need that level of care, would we have gone ahead with the relationship? Or would we have chosen to spare each other the profound levels of pain, tip our hats and wish each other luck on our path? I'm not sure either of us could answer that now. Illness becomes so intrinsically linked to everything around it that it's hard to imagine life without it.

You could say chronic illness is contagious – not in the literal sense, but in that everyone close to you becomes so thoroughly involved that they acquire a form of the illness themselves. It's not possible to see illness as living only in your body; the amount that it leaks into the lives of the people around you means that they too have to contend with it. They are eternal bystanders, cheering the sick person on, hoping that the good health achieved by one will be the good health of the other.

In an article for *Thrive Global,* Mary Wilson writes about becoming a carer for her husband, who had multiple medical conditions that he later died from: 'If you're going to be afraid of something, be afraid of how a loved one's chronic condition will affect both of you, and be afraid of what's happening with all of those people who have multiple chronic conditions and no caregiver, or a caregiver who also has multiple conditions.'

For a time I felt trapped. I wondered if my relationship with AJ, now built on a great dependence, might be more painful to keep than to lose. It's strange, but love, support and care from the people I loved sometimes felt like a knife in my heart, because I felt so utterly undeserving of it. How was it possible to take so much when I might never be able to give anything back? It's not as easy to accept love as you might think, especially if you feel that you are causing your loved ones pain. You are the hard conversation, the logistical issue in the day. You present to the people that you love a problem – one that they assure you they are bang-up for solving, or living with, but a problem nonetheless.

***

It was the afternoon and I was lying in my old childhood bedroom, surrounded by the spoils of a happy childhood: faded photos stuck to the wall, toys that I had held onto because I had felt responsible for their welfare, and old broken audio tapes that I'd recorded my voice onto, making up radio shows when I was eight. Embedded in each of these artefacts was a quiet hope that something good might be up ahead for me, a belief that if I worked hard enough and did the right things, I would be rewarded – maybe I'd get a good job, or live overseas.

But lying there that afternoon, the gaping hole that opened up between that time – when I would look out the window and daydream about what might come – and where I had found myself was profound. It seemed I wasn't ever going to be my old self again, or have the chance to live the adventurous, uninhibited life I'd hoped for. The Lolo Brothers wouldn't be caravanning around Australia or running off to live overseas on a whim – this operation had tied me to my home and my doctors indefinitely. I wouldn't have a marvellous career in media or teaching or anything that might satisfy me – I hadn't finished my degree, and even if I had, what workplace would ever want someone who needed as many sick days as I did?

And a family? That seemed more impossible than all the rest. That image I'd seen on the day I met AJ, the one of the child we would have together, now seemed foolish. The doctors had made it clear that the medication I was taking and the state of my body might make it difficult for me to fall pregnant.

The pain that was surging through me that day was not the type I was used to. It didn't come from raw nerve endings, and it wasn't a shot that emanated from my abdomen. Nor did it respond well to the techniques I had developed to deal with pain. I had tried to disperse it through me, to weaken it at its source, but the more I tried that, the bigger the ball of pain seemed to grow. It became clear that this pain was not of my body, but of my mind.

I lay there feeling utterly lost. It was as if I had been trudging through the snow, pulling my feet free as I went, and now I had found myself unable to move another step. I wasn't getting out of here. I had hit a dead-end. I couldn't imagine that the life ahead, full of pain and hospitals and drugs and needing help, could be anything but a burden for a partner like AJ.

It certainly wasn't a life that would have attracted an outsider. What use was I now? What purpose could I serve if my main function was to be cared for? My identity had become that of a sick person, and I didn't see the point in involving other people in its maintenance. It made more sense to quietly abandon my life and begin another one, deep underground, where I wouldn't let anyone down.

AJ and I had set up our new life in that tiny bedroom at the back of the house, the room where I had plotted and schemed my escape through my teenage years. He had been forced to rethink some of the plans he had been making to start his own studio, an expensive and time-consuming project. By this stage our relationship was well established and we had built a solid commitment, but we were still young and unprepared for a life of illness. Over those first few weeks out of hospital, the bedroom became suffocating. I hid in there, away from the prying and caring eyes of my family, unable to put on a brave face. It seemed clear to me that asking anyone who was not an immediate blood relative to care for me would be unfair. Asking anyone to share their life with me would be to clip their wings, and that was too great a responsibility.

Also, my anger was growing exponentially every day. I was angry that the illness had brought me to my knees and had exposed me in a way that I wasn't proud of. It brought my darkness out for all to see. It showed my weakness, my fear, my vanity. It strangled me and filled me so thoroughly that I could barely breathe. My temper was short. It wouldn't take much for the heat inside me to rise and for me to want to walk away from whatever had caused it. But nothing would release me from it, and as each day passed, the anger burned and grew. But no one could really confront it. It made sense that I would be angry, so my family quietly tolerated it. It was also too big now to take on.

But even though my anger would try to burn up anything that got in its way, the fact that everyone allowed it somehow enraged me even further.

When your anger starts to roam wildly, you have little power to stop it. You are left in its wake, watching, the stench of what it has burned filling your nostrils. And the more it destroys, the further you are pushed to the edges, away from the safe harbour of those that you love. Your anger becomes you. And it becomes impossible to know the difference between you and the anger that is using you as its vessel.

At the heart of my anger was not just that I had lost everything, but that I hadn't been given a fair chance to fight for it. Hadn't I done everything you're told to when you're young? I'd played the game by the rules and I'd still lost. If this was what could happen when you tried to live your life well, then there was no point to any of it.

***

Between visits from the nurse and the slow grind of routine – being showered, being toileted, being driven out – I began to plot an escape of a different kind. I had decided to find a way to live with the illness, but the only way I could see myself being able to do that, was by eradicating any remnant of that person I had been before, dreaming of a life that I might have had. It didn't all have to be lost. I could save those who had found themselves in my sinking vessel. It wasn't too late for them to jump free and swim for the shoreline that was slowly moving out of view.

So, one afternoon, I decided that I would ask AJ to leave me. It needed to be done in a way that meant no one would judge him – we would be able to work that out. I had a plan for that also, I would make sure that our friends and family knew that I had given him no choice. And with the pressure of him and the pressure to believe that I deserved to be loved gone, I began to plan a new life, hardening against the pain.

The day that I told AJ my plan, I felt almost excited. It's the sort of excitement that comes with knowing that you're close to the end of something exhausting. I imagined that this was how a runner might feel near the finishing line of a marathon, knowing the burning pain in their legs and the heaviness in their muscles will all soon be over. But unlike a marathon runner, who I imagined at least enjoyed their race, I was excited to be leaving everything behind. I would escape the weight of this guilt, the feeling of being a burden, and no one would need to bother about me again. The relief was exhilarating.

The 'asking AJ to leave me' plan wasn't as well executed as I had hoped. When I sat him down to discuss it, to make sure he knew that I had thought it through and that I knew it was the best plan for us, he just looked at me for a minute and shook his head.

'Nah,' he said. 'That's ridiculous.'

I was taken aback. I expected at least a couple of hours of conversation where we would go back and forth and finally come to an arrangement. But he didn't even entertain it for a moment. What I hadn't understood was that we had come too far now: this illness was no longer mine alone. I had no choice in that. The threads of this relationship weren't as easily broken as I had imagined. He had never imagined that this wasn't also his story. He made sure I understood that this hadn't happened to me, but to us. My story was now woven so completely into his and the people around me that it had also become theirs. This was no longer simply about me. And as much as it enraged me to know that I couldn't escape, I understood that I would need to accept the involvement of other people in this life. There was no longer a choice.

Slowly, only slightly to begin with, the anger started to recede. It started to return to its original state, back into deep sadness. And it was in the sadness that I began to rebuild. To find a way that I could dig my way upwards.

twelve

return to the world

The ileostomy started to reduce some of my abdominal symptoms, but the pain of the fistulas was still with me. I would carefully time taking my pain medication, pouncing on it the minute I was due. For weeks, I had been learning to live with the shock of seeing the inside of my body poking through my stomach. Each time I took a shower, I would hold onto the rail to steady myself. The first couple of weeks, I had to stop myself from being sick. An overwhelming fear of what my body might do had crept in and brought a hum that would grow louder each time I confronted my disfigured self.

There is something primal about the reaction to a changed body. Our bodies hold both the terror and the pleasure of human life, and when mine was cut and rearranged, the curtain was pulled away. I saw the folly of believing that my body would always be as it was. It felt like a betrayal in love. Why didn't I see it coming? Why did I ever believe my body was going to be faithful? I felt like a fool.

As Mildred Ngaage and Mark Agius describe in their study of the impact that scars have on self-image, a body that has been changed can result in the development of two separate selves:

'Following a critical incident, previously held beliefs about one's self are called into question and re-evaluated. A scar can be viewed as an intrusion – the barrier is no longer whole and one is left exposed. The change in appearance threatens sense of self and personhood. Patients must grieve for what has been lost and often there is a lack of continuity between the two self-images.'

I remember sitting on the edge of a hospital bed crying for what I saw as the loss of the self I was before the operation. I felt useless as this new version, in this new world. Embarrassed and useless. I had been conditioned to feel ashamed of this changed body. Everything that I was being told, was that I was less now. As Ngaage and Agius write, the skin is a barrier between the self and the world. When that has been ruptured, there is a sense of losing the wholeness of the self that existed before.

In the early days after the ileostomy operation, a nurse would come to the house to help me shower and teach me how to manage the stoma, the opening on my stomach that led to my bowel. Standing naked in front of another human, even when that human is a health professional, you are vulnerable. Reduced to your very basic self. Standing naked in front of nurses and doctors, you are reminded that your body is a specimen.

When she looked at me, she looked at what was wrong with me. She looked at how skinny I had become. She would talk to me about others she had showered who were in my position: 'You know,' she said once, 'there are men who have abused women through their stomas.' As she chatted on at full speed, without any comprehension for what she had said, I felt utterly shamed. I could be one of those women who had been disgraced. I had a body that people abused.

Vulnerability is a close bedfellow of shame. Vulnerability is the ledge on which you crouch, desperately clinging to the hope you won't be pushed into the abyss of shame. It is a place of painful anticipation.

The nurse could surely see my fear. She must have known of my vulnerability. I tried to hide all of these from her, to regain a foothold in our relationship, but I was exposed in every tentative move. I laughed at her jokes, I worked to make her feel good because I was deeply hopeful, perhaps even desperate, for her compassion. I yearned for her to sense my vulnerability and to tread gently. My humiliation. My shame. But I stood there in front of her as a specimen, as an illness categorisation, and my belief in my new-found uselessness was deepened.

After the showering, and learning how to care for the stoma, I would get dressed. Slowly at first. Tentatively. I was worried that I would knock something and hurt myself. I was scared of my body. My internal narrative became ferocious but pragmatic: *You are ugly and disfigured – get on with it.*

***

Graeme worked as a professional in a corporate environment, and had been struggling with an undiagnosed illness that meant he would often be caught by a sudden, urgent need to urinate. If he didn't find a toilet, his bladder would empty of its own accord. For fourteen years, he went from doctor to doctor trying to find out what was wrong. For years he was misdiagnosed with interstitial cystitis, then finally with bladder cancer. It wasn't until the cancer diagnosis that he received therapy that helped with his symptoms. But until then, Graeme lived with this enormous secret, which he was forced to find ways to hide from the people that he worked with:

'It came right down to the fact that when I was at work I used to get up and go down to the toilet, and people sitting within eyesight of the toilet door, you know, that girl or that guy ... they're gonna see me going in so many times today. To me, [I imagined] they were like, 'Graeme's going in again, that's number six of the day and it's not even lunchtime yet.' It really got to me. I used to resort to going to one toilet, then when I had to go again, I'd go to the other side of the floor.'

When Graeme told me this, it took my breath away. I had done the same thing for years. I would make sure no one saw me go in or leave the bathroom. I told him we were the same, and we both stopped for a moment. And for me at least, it felt enormously comforting to know that someone else had lived in this same darkness as I had. The secrecy can feel lonely.

Like Graeme, Meg Rodriguez found that hiding a chronic illness from close friends became a daily habit, as she described in an article in *Medium*, 'Sick and Sick of pretending':

'You barely slept last night, you're exhausted, and your body hurts – but you'd never tell your friend those things. You don't want to be known as the girl who always cancels plans. Instead, you did your hair, and you put on makeup. You covered up the dark bags under your eyes – an art you've now perfected. And you manage to float through your hour-long coffee date, never even letting on that you're sick. It's because you've chosen to wear the mask that says "everything is fine".'

I would always end any discussion I had with friends or family with, 'but I'm fine'. And I hoped that I would be believed and left alone because I didn't want anyone to assume that I wasn't in control of my illness and how it was impacting me. I feared that my autonomy would be encroached upon as it sometimes had in my work. It felt vital that people around me believed I could cope.

When you do disclose the true impact of your illness to someone, asking them to understand and possibly support you, sometimes they start to believe they have a say in how you manage that illness. If you're judged to be eating the wrong food, or pushing yourself too hard, or any number of transgressions, then it feels as if the contract between 'sick' person and 'caring other' has been violated. The sense is that if you're going to talk about how sick you are, then you'd best be doing something about it – or at the very least not be seen to be making it worse with questionable life choices.

This is partly why, for many people with chronic illness, non-disclosure or partial disclosure seems the safest route.

Another reason is that an admittance of illness can be treated with hostile scepticism. Often when we first learn that someone is sick, or we read about their stories, our first impulse is to question their claims. Are they being hysterical? Do they feel sorry for themselves? Are they asking for sympathy when it's not deserved?

Reports on this sort of reaction from the community come largely from young people and especially from young women. In her book *Invisible: How Young Women with Serious Health Issues Navigate Work, Relationships, and the Pressure to Seem Just Fine* Michele Lent Hirsch investigated this issue: 'When a fistful of serious health issues struck me in my twenties, I saw how being young and female was inextricably linked to my experience.' Michele goes on, throughout her book, to describe the experience of not looking how you are feeling. Being young and feminine, the ultimate symbol of vivacity, makes a story of pain and suffering a hard sell.

This instinct to avoid admitting to your pain is common among young women. I reached out to Olivia when I saw her Instagram post about chronic illness on Tiddas 4 Tiddas, an online initiative designed to empower young black women. She shared a brief part of her experience of endometriosis, and how her long search for a diagnosis began with a presumption that her painful periods should be just 'sucked up': 'I remember when we were learning about menstruation at school the teacher said, "Period pain is not a valid reason to miss a day of school."' After enduring pain for years, she finally admitted she couldn't handle it anymore and found help. More recently, she felt compelled to tell her story so that more young girls know they should be heard: 'Educate yourself on your body, challenge things you feel aren't right, don't ever doubt yourself and what you are going through...'

Men often deal with different cultural codes around masculinity and illness, but these make disclosure equally difficult. In a study from East Tennessee University, researcher Matthew Daggett explores the intersection between illness disclosure and masculine culture:

> 'Men who encounter chronic illness within their lives will engage in identity management to maintain a hegemonic masculine identity – especially when disclosing. They will try to preserve their sense of self by giving others the perception that they are leading normal lives despite their various illnesses.'

Pressure to conform to dominant identity structures, means that disclosure either won't happen or will be controlled to still fit with socially designed ideals of strength and stoicism. Often, it's too draining to attempt to challenge masculine stereotypes while sick. Easier to conform quietly and to live with an illness in secret.

***

It was the first time I had left the house since the ileostomy operation. Going to a pub to see music was the first defiant act of normalcy: a statement to everyone, and especially to myself, that the surgery and what I saw as my body disfigured, hadn't changed the me within. I wanted to resume my old life. My ileostomy bag was attached to my stomach, and as it was large enough to sit on my upper thigh I had to choose my outfit carefully to disguise it. I needed to know I could play the role.

AJ and I walked into the pub as we had always done, and our friends greeted us as if we had returned from a long trip. This ritual of meeting friends and seeing music was an important part of who we were, finally being returned to us. But not long after we arrived, I was laughing with a friend when I felt something growing wet on my leg. That feeling immediately became a tornado as my body rushed with humiliation. I stopped laughing and moved away suddenly; I looked for AJ in the darkness and the chaos, becoming frantic.

I reached down and felt the fabric becoming soaked beneath my fingers. The ileostomy bag had broken, and its shameful contents were slowly seeping through my clothing and running down my leg. My stomach lurched. My mind raced. Panic. It wasn't shameful simply because of the experience itself – being covered in my own effluent – but because I had been foolish enough to want to be normal. What was I thinking?

It is at moments like this when shame is at its most dangerous, teetering into self-loathing. Tara Brach, founder and senior teacher of the Insight Meditation Community of Washington DC, describes the experience of shame as circular, something that winds back and becomes a weapon we use against ourselves:

> 'When inevitable pain arises, we take it personally. We are diagnosed with a disease or go through a divorce, and we perceive that we are the cause of unpleasantness (we're deficient) or that we are the weak and vulnerable victim (still deficient). Since everything that happens reflects on me, when something seems wrong, the source of wrong is me.'

The humiliation of that evening struck a decisive blow against my connection to the rest of the world. I didn't know anyone else who this might happen to. I didn't know anyone who wouldn't be frightened or repulsed by it. I could see the attempts of friends to hide their discomfort. They moved back slightly and changed their faces. I saw the horror flash behind their eyes.

Aloneness is distinct from loneliness. Aloneness is the perception that you are experiencing something completely by yourself. It is the feeling that you are isolated from the shared understanding that underscores most experiences. You feel as though you are watching from a window as everyone else moves through life. Aloneness for me was having insufficient language to explain the layers of hurt that I felt in that moment. I was lost. I grabbed AJ, hiding myself as much as I could, and we rushed home.

This was the first of many such experiences, and in time I began to call certain friends to talk through each embarrassing event. It was almost like it needed to be witnessed to be believed.

My body was out of my control. Is it a basic, primal need to master our bodies? If we step out beyond chronic illness for a moment, we see a society drenched in secrecy and shame surrounding our bodily functions. We are embarrassed when even our normal bodily functions shift from private to public space – think of the shame of a teenage girl when her menstrual blood is exposed. There is a relationship between this shame and shame we feel when our illness symptoms are exposed.

'I am ashamed of being sick,' wrote Angelika Byczkowski, a woman with Ehlers-Danlos syndrome, in her article 'In today's society, chronic illness is viewed as a personal failing':

'I spent my previous life trying to prove how tough I was, declared my independence early, made my own way successfully, and now I've lost it all.

'In our competitive society, chronic infirmity or illness is viewed as a personal failing rather than the random stroke of fate that it is. If my pain and disability were temporary, I would get sympathy and accommodation, but incurable suffering makes most people uncomfortable. They become impatient and distant, and I detect an undercurrent of belief that I must have done something to deserve this – something they can avoid doing.'

Shame also comes when we open ourselves up in the hope of compassion. It is a painful surrendering of power to seek understanding from others. The risk we take is that we will be denied, or it will be fumbled and the opportunity lost. And for so many, the risk of being denied compassion is far more painful than not receiving it at all.

Many people struggle to react helpfully or sensitively to someone talking about their chronic illness. Fundamentally, this kind of conversation is an uncomfortable reminder of the flawed human condition, and we instinctively categorise and compare in order to manage difficult ideas. But when someone tries to compare your experience of illness to somebody else's, you often feel reduced to generalities. 'My sister has stopped eating meat and her Crohn's disease is now under control,' is the kind of response that erases the individual's unique experience. It also sets up false expectations, ones that only compound that feeling of shame when they aren't met. These conversations can be extremely painful for someone with a chronic illness.

So often when the leap of faith fails, and the attempt to explain your illness to someone falls flat, the division between the self and the rest of the world deepens.

How do you live in a world that doesn't understand the pain that you feel, the fear that underscores your day or the instability that now dominates your decision-making? In the months after my ileostomy I had to accept that I had hit rock bottom and the outside world could never truly understand what I was going through.

But surprisingly, finally realising this was a relief. I had great support and love from my friends and my family, but I was alone in this experience, and instead of fearing that aloneness, I had to embrace it.

This realisation was the start of finding a way through shame. It was clear to me early on that one of the mechanisms of shame is secrecy. Keeping a secret is a tiring and demeaning existence. In 1993, John Bradshaw wrote a seminal work on shame called *Healing the Shame that Binds You,* in which he explains the relationship between shame and secrecy:

> 'Shame becomes toxic because of premature exposure. We are exposed either unexpectedly or before we are ready to be exposed. We feel helpless and powerless. No wonder then that we fear the scrutinising eyes of others. However, the only way out of toxic shame is to embrace the shame – we must come out of hiding.'

Shame must be combated from the inside. The trick is to find confidence in your own story. You have to allow yourself to experience illness in its full breadth, without seeking permission from the outside world. I realised that I'd been seeking permission at every turn. I didn't believe

I was entitled to comfort. For years I had been seen by Dr Jeff, and when he became too popular for me to see him whenever I needed to, I began to see another doctor at the same practice as well. Dr Catherine Lazaroo was friends with Dr Jeff and cut from the same cloth. Like him, she took the time to understand me beyond my illness and saw me struggling with the fact I wasn't coping. It took her sort of sensitivity and insight to give me the permission I so desperately sought. She looked at me and told me that I was sick. That my sickness was profound and debilitating and that if I was suffering as a result, that that was normal. I could let a breath out. It was okay that I wasn't okay.

***

After living with my parents for several months, AJ and I finally moved into our own home. We had been so well cared for by my parents, but it felt as if we were living shadow lives. Even though I wasn't quite ready to move out and try to make enough of a living to get by, we couldn't stay any longer; we had been independent for too much of our lives to go back. Our new place was a tiny house that barely had room for a couch or our bed, and I spent long days cooped up, pacing its old carpeted floors. The air in the small space became thick with the smell of illness.

With each breath I felt like I was exhaling a blackness into the house. I knew I wouldn't be able to escape this for some time, and the house wrapped around me like a swaddle. It began to feel a little like hospital, with a cycle of sameness and routines that tricked me into believing that I was safe. I started to doubt I would survive if I left its confines.

For many, many months that was all that I needed to fill my days. I would spend the daylight moving from the couch to the bed to sitting on the one chair that was tucked neatly under the kitchen table. The days were endless, and it became a test of endurance. I had to keep going; there was no getting off.

I would look to anything to take my mind away from my body and the ileostomy bag. I would watch television endlessly. I had developed a reliance on the way the programming marked the shifts in my day. Early-morning talk shows with anxiety-inducing paid advertising, then cooking shows, Oprah Winfrey and daytime soaps. Before mobile phones were there to take us away from ourselves, television was the drug of choice. It became easy to shut myself down with this old form of distraction.

And what I was distracting myself from was how sick I was, with aches that clubbed my body and persistent pain in my abdomen. But it was also about the unwanted lodger taking up residence on my body. It was hard to accept the ileostomy bag, living on me like a leech. I was afraid to go swimming because I was pretty sure it would come unstuck, and I had to make sure the foods I ate weren't too gassy or too fibrous. Gassy foods would enlarge the bag without warning, and too much fibre could mean another obstruction. But it had to be a secret: that was the social contract that I had unwittingly signed. I would work hard to find different ways to hide it under my clothing, finding outfits that would gather in such a way that only a keen eye would detect it. I had to carefully choose something that wasn't tight around my stomach or the lower half of my body. Jeans were out. Stockings were very difficult. I felt the hum of shame every time I dressed. If I leaned too far in one direction, or moved too quickly, would something protrude? Would I be found out? Would someone see that I had something that I didn't want them to see?

Clothing offers the possibility of presenting like you are normal. Paula P is the founder of clothing site 'My Chronic Style', dedicated to women who live with invisible illnesses. Living herself with endometriosis, adenomyosis, fibromyalgia and chronic fatigue syndrome, she created this business because she wanted to address the difficulties of getting up, washed and dressed every day. For many people who suffer from illnesses such as fibromyalgia, clothing itself can cause pain. As described by one member of @themighty, an online support hub for people with illness and their carers, fibromyalgia is 'like every part of your body is bruised but [the bruises] are invisible, and sometimes you wish they were visible because then people might take your pain seriously'. For people with these kinds of chronic illness, even the armour is too painful to wear.

I don't think I would have ever been a poster girl for the wearing of an ileostomy bag. They required too much maintenance to avoid breaking. The unexpected shifts and changes in my body, too easily filled them with air, and if I didn't change the base plate frequently it would fall off with little warning. I spent too many nights waking in fright to find the ileostomy contents seeping out all over me and the bed. AJ and I would jump up in a daze and clean up the mess. We eventually became a skilled team at this kind of clean-up, like scrubbing down a crime scene. If only it was a sport, we would have been competitive. In a half-awake state one of us would grab the soiled sheets and bundle them into the washing machine while the other found clean sheets to cover the bed. If you'd walked into the room after the event, you would never have guessed what had happened only moments before. We would move wordlessly through that tiny house, aware of the trauma that this was causing us but unable to deal with it in the middle of that darkness, in the middle of the night.

Next we would need to clean *me* up. I would turn on the shower to wash myself while AJ cut and prepared a new ileostomy bag to be stuck to my skin. I hated every moment. But I couldn't. I couldn't scream and shake my fists at the sky. There was no time for those sorts of feelings. Instead we would quietly return to bed and try to dream it away, as if the problem could disappear when light came.

In the morning, we would half-heartedly try to console each other. I would feel bereft, but there was barely room to surrender to how difficult this was. It happened so often that there was no point in raging against it. AJ never made me feel like it was hard for him, or that I was disgusting. Actually, the opposite. And I knew intellectually that I shouldn't be ashamed, but my heart burned at the thought that I could be reduced to this child who couldn't control her body. I felt humiliated.

Some days I would walk up to the shops to sit in an old Italian bakery and spend an unjustifiable amount of time searching the crowd for someone that might be like me. It's absurd, really, but I thought I'd be able to tell if someone was hiding the same secret as me. I would search people's faces then shoot a quick look at their leg. Was that a bulge?

I did find a woman in my neighbourhood who I was sure had one. Based on absolutely nothing, I cased her for months. I watched how she moved down the street. I tried to see what she bought at the chemist. Whenever she was looking away I would stare at her body, and I grew in my confidence that she was like me. I even tried to catch her eye so that I could tell her somehow, wordlessly, that we were the same. I'm almost ashamed of that time, so desperate was I to share this with someone that I made it up. Luckily, she had no idea that I had been analysing her, trying to guess what might have been happening beneath her clothing. How terrible that she should bear this storyline that I'd forced onto her.

Hiding my own ileostomy bag became an occupation in itself. The bag clinging to my leg would expand with liquid very quickly. I was alert, waiting for something horrible to happen. And it often did.

I could not keep this a secret any more. I decided that I would tell anyone who enquired about my health that my ileostomy bag was there beneath my clothes. It was in part about control, making sure that I was the one who told the story, but it was also about showing that I was not ashamed. Some people recoiled visibly and some covertly. Others told me they couldn't talk to me about it because it made them uncomfortable. But for many more, it removed a barrier that had been between us. The more I projected a comfort with it, the more people around me seemed at ease. But beneath my confidence I was constantly embarrassed. I felt like a joke.

***

AJ and I slowly continued to rebuild our lives. It became clear it was a life that had asked a lot of our relationship. But while the wild winds had certainly knocked us off course, we were proud of how far we had come. Pulling in sails, we had found how to move safely with each other in those rough waters. We had kept our little boat afloat. We often talked about that woman with red lipstick who told us our relationship wouldn't survive, and we would make fun of the moment, and how shocking we had found the exchange. Out of nowhere, one of us would quote her to make the other laugh: 'You are destined to fail,' one of us would say, re-enacting her stern tone. And we laughed knowing that we had both resolved to make her a liar.

One night, sitting outside our new home in our old Valiant VE, we were talking about what we had been through. And as the sun set over an old factory roof at the end of our street, AJ asked me to marry him. It was a moment of rebellion – defiance of the idea that we would only survive 'against all odds'. It was a question that instead made a statement about us clear: we were going to do this together. And I said yes, in the same spirit.

In the coming months we planned a wedding, and my mum made me a dress that would hide the colostomy bag. We would be married in the church that both my grandparents and my parents had been married in, surrounded by people who would join us in our grand rebellion. On the morning of our wedding, as AJ and I sat together before heading off to our ceremony in our Valiants, we both started singing at the same time, a song that Reggie had sung to all his grandkids as children – a song AJ had learned when he had joined our family: 'She's a pretty little dear, she lives uptown/her daddy is a butcher, his name is Brown...' The only explanation I can find for the fact that we had started an obscure song midway through at precisely the same time, is that Reggie was there, whispering it into our ears.

I was him and he was me. Our lives intertwined.

thirteen

the impossible becomes real

The days in that tiny house ran into each other as I shifted from one brief, crazy part-time job to another, interspersed with periods of intense sickness. So reliable was that feeling of endlessness that I didn't imagine much would change anytime soon.

I should have remembered that the only thing that was reliable was how quickly and unexpectedly the carpet could be pulled from underneath you.

It was 2003, an afternoon before I was due to go back to hospital for yet another attempt to clear away the damage that the fistulas had wreaked upon me. Two years on from the ileostomy, the abscesses were still causing issues that needed colorectal surgery. Almost every six weeks I would go into hospital and be put under a general anaesthetic so that the infection could be cleared. The daily pain of the abscesses was intense, but so too was the invasion of each surgery, and the energy that it took to recover from what was a pretty simple procedure.

That afternoon I was passing the time at home, vacuuming that lounge-room floor. It's a part of the memory of this moment that has always remained vivid. Vacuuming is surely one of the most mundane tasks there is, but when you are doing something mundane and something extraordinary happens, the extraordinary somehow becomes even more luminous. Ever since this day, vacuuming has been imbued with a kind of magic for me.

I was working my way around a pretty small lounge room, doing anything but thinking about the job at hand. It was around 5pm, so once I finished this task I would get ready for the next day in hospital. Pack a little bag. Choose a book to read. Pack a stash of extra ileostomy bags. I would put on the Sonic Youth album *Daydream Nation* and get lost in the drone and the movement of it that never failed to take me somewhere better. And as is normally the case when you vacuum, part of the enjoyment (if you can ever see it that way) is that it allows you to drift away. The squeal of the motor would become the soundtrack to daydreams that lifted me out of wherever I was and into somewhere entirely different – the future, the past, alternative universes, anywhere but the present. But that afternoon, as the sun was about to set, was different.

This daydream began as they regularly did, in the ordinary. I thought about the operation. Would my surgeon be there as normal? What time would I need to wake up? I remembered the last time I had gone in to hospital and began wondering if I could handle it better this time. And then my mind drifted further from reality, where the daydreams grow wilder. While I thought about what might go wrong that following day, I had one of those random wonderings: *what would it be like to be unaware that you were pregnant before you had this sort of invasive procedure?* And from that tiny provocation, my wonderings expanded. Really, what would it be like? To participate in something without being aware of the real cost? What would happen if, during and because of a procedure, you lost a baby you never knew you had?

The living room was clean, and as I clicked the vacuum off, the daydream faded into the background and I snapped back to where I was standing on that ratty carpet. And without much further contemplation, my feet took me to the door and down the road to the chemist on the corner of my street. I had no reason to believe that I might have a baby that would be in danger if I had an operation the next day, because my illness and the drugs that I was on virtually made that impossible. But my feet still took me into the chemist, and I dutifully bought a pregnancy test.

I was like many women who find themselves dealing with a likelihood that they will never have children, children they may have longed for since they were children themselves. The illness was unrelenting and it didn't look like I would be in a state of health for some time, so I had been dealing with the possibility that getting pregnant might not ever be possible for me.

This is the case for so many people with chronic illness who had hoped to have children. Not only are you dealing with the impact that the illness has on you and your hopes, but you must also accept some direct and lasting impacts on the people around you: your partner will not have a baby, your parents will never be grandparents.

Sherri and her husband Michael were sure they wanted to spend the rest of their lives together. After much deliberation and long conversations, they decided that they would like to ensure that, after the rigours of cancer treatment, they would have the option to have a family one day. As they were about to undergo IVF to store eggs, Sherri's cancer diagnosis suddenly became one that needed immediate chemotherapy, which meant they were unable to go through an IVF cycle, the first round of which they had booked in for the following week. It was an abrupt end to any hope that they might have a family, as Sherri explained:

'Being infertile is difficult for both of us. Not being able to make the decision about whether we want to have children ourselves [has been devastating]. He feels guilty that he wasn't able to make a decision about having children soon enough and that we didn't have kids before I got sick. I'm a bit more of an optimist but I was devastated.'

I asked Sherri how long it had taken her to come to terms with not being able to have children; she took a breath: 'I'm still working through that.' She is pretty sure that of everything that she has endured as a result of her lung cancer, coping with her infertility has been the hardest.

When I think back to why I got that pregnancy test that day, I struggle to find a definite reason. Part of it may have been looking for distraction. I would find myself doing strange things, so that the strangeness would be the focus and overwhelm the task ahead. Something that would keep my mind busy. Something to entertain me. And perhaps it was also a way to keep alive this idea of having a baby, when the likelihood seemed like it was ever diminishing.

But that doesn't explain it, and I have never sufficiently answered what it was that day that made me think about a baby.

About our baby.

I took the pregnancy test and waited, playing the game as if it were real. Thrilled to be doing something I had only really seen done on television. It was fun to believe for those small moments that something like this could be possible for me, for us, for my entire family. Then two little lines appeared on the test. There was a baby inside me, tucked away, willing to take life on. Willing to be ours.

Whenever I'm asked, in questionnaires or games played with friends, to speak about the favourite day of my life, this was that day. It was a day that proved you can't rely only on what you believe about your future, because I couldn't have imagined this for me. I was too scared. It shook my foundations, which were already unstable, but this time it shook them in the best way.

I rang AJ, who was at work, and tried to tell him, but the words were absurd. 'Sit down, I can't prepare you for what I'm about to say, but whatever you're doing, you need to cancel it, because I can't sit here alone with this news...' I tried to explain to him the nonsense that we were having a baby, and while he didn't understand fully, he understood enough to feel the excitement of what this meant.

Just as I had begun to mourn the loss of the children we probably wouldn't have, the world had flipped on itself. Now, after the work AJ and I had put into reforming our relationship, our life together, we had to bring another life into it. I became nervous at how much I wanted this. I had become accustomed to the idea that things could go wrong. I urgently got in touch with my doctors at the hospital and told them what I had just found out. They were as shocked as I was, and we all scurried around trying to work out what we would do next. The operation was cancelled and we adjusted my medication to avoid potential harm to the baby.

I was allocated a specialist gynaecologist who, though she had not seen this sort of thing before up close and personal, had done some extra study and felt confident about seeing me through the pregnancy. I also visited an ileostomy specialist in a cancer ward who gave me pamphlets on the worst possible outcome. It wasn't pretty.

When I was young and wondering if I would one day become a mum, this wasn't what I had imagined.

I had to fathom the grand responsibility of bringing a child into the world via a sick and unreliable vessel. The fear woke me up early the next morning like a shot of reality. How were we going to do this? I had no idea how I might manage such a massive task in the state I was in.

So it was with a wild mix of fear and excitement that I stepped off the precipice and into the unknown world of having a baby while dealing with the challenge and uncertainty of illness. If AJ and I could get away with this, it seemed we would have beaten the odds. We spent sleepless nights trying to come to terms with the sudden twist of luck, waking each other up to talk through all the questions that sprang into our minds.

But the nine months were a tortuous and long wait for something to go wrong. After you've had illness for a while, you come to expect things to go wrong, and this was no different, except this time it was more painful as it involved someone who had been innocent to this whole business. What I did enormously enjoy, though, were the moments that many pregnant women experience – when people felt my stomach uninvited. Whenever it happened, it was with great joy that I let them know they had just gently caressed my ileostomy. This baby had no idea what they had signed up to.

A study on 'Pregnancy with Chronic Illness' explored these complexities:

> 'The experience of pregnancy with a chronic illness is one of a balancing act between the fantasy of being normal and living with the ever-present demands of a chronic condition. Women deal with the physical and emotional demands by managing the blessings and burdens created by the symptoms of pregnancy, placing in perspective the worry that this creates and actively managing the constant flow of information.
>
> 'Symptom management, always important, becomes imbued with new meaning: "If my disease flares, what will happen to the baby?" A hyper-awareness of bodily changes intensifies, and worry over what is occurring or could occur in the body increases maternal stress. Pregnancy can be experienced as a waiting game rather than as an enjoyable time of being with one's child, with the chronically ill mother counting the days until the baby is out of her body and "safe".'

***

Fear, untamed, can take you out so far from shore that you begin to panic. You do whatever you can to control the storyline, and if that means getting ahead of the storyline, well, all the better. I spent hours poring over websites detailing any experience that might resemble mine, just so that I would be prepared. But those websites were never really helpful, and often had me holding on for dear life in the early hours of the morning as I flicked through image after image of stomas that had distended. Gruesome stuff, really. Not for the faint-hearted. But when you're scared, you feel like the more you know, the less likely the chance of a surprise attack.

For both AJ and I, the pregnancy was a series of careful steps. We tiptoed into each month, hoping that if we were quiet enough, no one would notice. When you're frightened, everything you look at is seen through the prism of fear, and you eventually forget what started the fear in the first place. It just ends up being an ugly feeling in the pit of your stomach that accompanies you everywhere, making you wonder if buying food at the grocery store is actually scary or if there is something else at play. But trying to keep that fear contained to its real source is difficult. Like riding a wild horse, you can't really dictate where fear will take you; you just have to hold on.

I had made careful plans with the doctors involved about what would happen at the birth.

Because of the perianal infection, I needed to have a caesarean section, and that meant that along with a gastroenterologist I needed to have a bowel surgeon on call, in case something went wrong when they cut me open.

So many plans were made and so much detail discussed before we landed on a date that suited everyone. We were going to be ready to get my baby out safely. My gastroenterologist was a wild and confident doctor with blazing red hair that gave her a heroic aura – in the style of a warrior in *Braveheart*. I possibly read a little too much into her confidence, but that was what mattered to me. I wanted people who could tell me that we were all going to get out of this adventure alive.

But maybe fear has some power over the world. How else can you explain the fact that, with all the preparations in place, the caesarean booked in and the doctors confident that the pregnancy would go to plan, the baby came two weeks early? How else can you explain the fact that 'two weeks early' landed on the Easter long weekend, when virtually every doctor in town was away?

I was pottering around my house when my waters broke. This wasn't the plan. I wasn't supposed to go into labour at *all*. AJ was out walking his mum's dog in a suburb half an hour away and no one could get in touch with him. I had to race to hospital with some friends and hope that he would find out soon enough that his baby was on its way.

I arrived at hospital to learn that every one of the doctors I'd been consulting with – the bowel doctors and my specialist gynaecologist, who had spent weeks mapping out how they would manage the birth – was unavailable. The hospital staff rang down the list, but everyone was out of town for Easter.

The doctor on the ward that day had an unkempt grey moustache and a messy mop of hair that was barely contained by a surgical cap. He came into the room where I was being assessed looking like he'd just rolled out of bed. He looked at me, then at my file, and then at me again and scratched his stubbled chin.

'I'm not sure how we're going to do this,' he said cutely. He continued to scratch his chin and stare into the middle distance. I lay there looking at him in disbelief. Hadn't this guy been to medical school? Hadn't his family made countless sacrifices to get him there? Didn't his spouse say goodbye to him at the door each morning in the full belief that he was what he said he was – a freaking doctor? What the hell right did he have to stand in front of me and scratch his goddamn chin?

Had I not been so afraid that I might scare off my only remaining hope, I would have screamed at him to get the hell away from me. But I didn't. I lay there as other staff tried to make enough noise to cover up what had just happened. But when he touched me, my body lurched involuntarily. I was angry that he suddenly had so much power over me and the rest of my life. Our life. I was angry because I had no choice but to trust him, and I resented how easily he assumed that I *would* just trust him. But it was a familiar hospital experience. I was at a crossroads in my life, hoping to be joined by a new member of our family, and the doctor was simply at work.

AJ ran into the room panting. This was not going to be the quiet night in with takeaway he had envisaged. He could see that I was worried about what was happening. He was worried too, but did everything in his power to hide it from me.

Fear descended on me like it had never before: true, full-scale, mortal fear. The sort of fear where your mouth empties of liquid and you think you may vomit at any moment. I'd felt fear often enough in the past, but this time, it was not for me; it was for my unborn child. How was I going to get my baby here safely? With this broken body covered in surgery scars that even cutting my abdomen would be particularly difficult?

At the very best of times, birth is a miraculous beating of the odds. For anyone in the midst of it, there's always a profound feeling of walking a tightrope. The confidence behind all the cute presents that were given to you at the baby shower, and the games you played with your partner to come up with a baby name, and the miniature clothes you arranged in a drawer, suddenly feels utterly foolish. Of course things go wrong. Of course giving birth forces you to confront mortality, no matter how easy the pregnancy or healthy the mother.

What chronic illness added to this equation was a particularly grave sense of responsibility, because I already knew how terribly things could go wrong. But ultimately it was out of my hands. It was in the hands of a doctor who wasn't quite sure what he was doing. It was in the hands of the world.

An overly conscientious anaesthetist decided that I would need to be knocked out for the birth – something to do with the perianal fistulas. This wasn't in our original plan. I hadn't imagined that I wouldn't be conscious for the birth. But everything was happening so quickly, and she had concerns about infection causing serious issues. She looked at me with concerned eyes and told me it was for the best, then grabbed my hand in a familiar grasp as she tried to console me. I wouldn't be there, awake, for the birth, and because I was going under a general anaesthetic, AJ couldn't be in the room. I would be in The Nothingness, and my baby would arrive without their mother or her father there to greet them.

As they wheeled me in, I desperately grabbed at AJ's hand and tried to hold on. I don't know what I thought would happen. Maybe I was trying to pull myself off the bed, to make a last-minute escape. Maybe I was trying to take myself out of there altogether, right back to when I was a child and I believed that a body was just that – a simple machine that did what it was asked. Maybe I wanted to go back even further, back to when I was born into this body. Maybe if I had done some things differently, I don't know what, maybe it wouldn't be like this – with our baby trying to enter the world all alone.

The nurses gathered around my head and tried to make me smile. The anaesthetist told me to look at my hand as soon as I woke up because she would write the time that the baby was born there. And as she gave me the anaesthetic, I looked around the room and begged them all to do their best job. Trusting these people was all I could do.

My eyes closed, and I went into The Nothingness. I didn't dream of my baby, because you can't dream of anything there. I was straddling two worlds, and so was my child, both of us between the living and the dead. While the doctors worked, I was out at sea, with no idea if land would come into view. But then, just like that, I could see the tip of something. A hill. It dipped out of view again, and I stared at it for so long that my eyesight became blurry. Then, without warning, it bobbed up again, and this time stayed in view for just a bit longer. It was land. And just like that, I felt consciousness grabbing me by the scruff of my neck and pulling me up. I opened my eyes with everything I had and, though it felt like concrete, I pulled my hand to my face.

The words, *8.49 Girl* was scrawled on my hand. She had made it, all by herself.

It would be reasonable to assume that the moment of knowing that she had arrived would be joyful. But mostly I felt a tremendous grief, deep and immovable. Life could be so dangerous, and there was little I could do to keep that danger from coming all the way into my home. And now there was one more innocent person living there with me. It hurt to know that the world could be this callous and hard. That everything gained needed to be done through deals and at all costs.

After giving birth, a particular quote kept coming to my mind. I had heard it some years earlier, at the funeral of a friend's father who'd died of a heart attack. My friend and I had been in our very early twenties, and it was inconceivable to us that her dad could have left for a run one day and simply never returned home. It had taken the entire family unawares; no one had imagined that the rest of their lives would be sculpted from that day and the devastating loss it brought. When my friend's mum spoke, I saw a tiny glimpse into the life of a woman who had lost her everything, something I had not seen before. She quoted Shakespeare's Cleopatra at the loss of Antony: 'Now I am no more than a woman, ruled by the same lowly passion as the maid who milks and does the humblest chores. I might now hurl my sceptre at the destructive gods and tell them that this earthly world was as good as their heavenly one, until they stole away its jewel, Antony.' It came to me as I lay there looking at my hand, how easily these jewels can be taken away from us. How merciless the world seems when you are standing at the door between the living and the dead.

***

I was the last one to meet her. For an hour or so, an entire room of friends and family passed her from one to the other, kissing her and welcoming her like she was royalty. AJ held her, like the golden prize she was. He had been left in a different sort of nothingness, waiting for her to emerge from behind the operating theatre doors. And as she was passed to him, in a dark hallway, he was first to meet the child that he had always loved – she was now safely in his arms. Children should always be greeted with the maximum song and dance when they enter the world – I have a friend whose partner wore a tuxedo for an entire week as he waited for their daughter to arrive because he wanted to be dressed appropriately. When my daughter arrived there was an entire waiting room of people crying and laughing because she had arrived. Everyone came out to meet her and she was worth the trip. She was beautiful.

When I was wheeled out through the corridors and back to the ward a couple of hours later, I could hear her, lungs full and calling for me. We had been calling for each other. And when she was finally handed to me, I didn't understand her. I couldn't work her out. I couldn't see clearly where she began and where I ended. When I held her for that first time, I was confused – was she me? Was I her? We had been one thing for so long, was it now that we became two?

***

As my daughter rested on my chest, I wondered if she knew anything. What had she arrived with? Was it a blank page, or was she already scribbling away with everything she had already learned on her journey here? Did she already understand that life is travelled on the thinnest of wires, and that the smallest of winds can blow you away? I looked into her eyes, and felt like I saw her years from now. AJ and I still maintain that when we held her that first time, she told us who she was.

But I was sore and needed to be sick. The enormity of her arrival and the doubt I'd had in my ability to bring her here safely had ripped me apart. The fear that I had felt in those final moments had shaken me to my core. I couldn't bear how hard this world was, and as she looked up at me, I wondered if I had finally been beaten. I felt a rush of panic, and the anger that had greeted me on my arrival back from The Nothingness was simmering away inside me.

Was I going to be able to do this? Could I carve away some of the fear that had calcified on my body?

Giving birth changed me, and the change lasted inside me for years. I was on high alert. Staying in the hospital that first night as a mother, when I could hardly move, was frightening. When my ileostomy bag broke, I had to call maternity nurses – who were unaccustomed to this sort of thing – to help clean me up. Feeling as helpless as the baby I was trying to hold was excruciating.

But as her small hand found its way to mine, I was reminded of the hands that had held mine three years before, when I was sick in that hospital bed. I was transported back to that moment, when the world had seemed so hard but also finally made sense, and it struck me that I had known how to do this all along.

***

I have often asked people who have been through illness or a hardship of one type or another, was there a moment when everything changed? When suddenly, all the pain and all the struggle fell away. Or at least, when you shifted just slightly, out of the shadows, and the sunlight caught your face. And often there is a moment.

I had one.

Not that day, holding her hand, but not so long after that it couldn't be seen as connected. I was back at home and lying next to her. For weeks, I had been consumed by the worries that a new baby brings, as well as those around my health, an ever-evolving problem. And with the ileostomy bag and a caesarean to recover from, I was sore and constantly reminded that I was unusual.

The moment, on one level, was mundane. On another, a profound experience of acceptance, an acceptance that reverberated right through me, from deep in my past and right into a future, where I could picture a life that was okay – where we were okay. To be fair to this moment, it likely didn't arrive out of nowhere. More likely, it had been building for some time and was the composite of the many, many moments that had come before it.

Lying there, I suddenly knew that if I continued to sink into the worry and pain of my illness, weighed down by disbelief and anguish over how my body had been hurt, then I might never come back up. The only way through was to accept that I had fallen, and no amount of anger or resistance was going to get me up again. Anger had felt like the only satisfactory response. I had believed that anything less would undermine the horror of my experiences. But anger had started to become a way of being. In that moment, I felt like I was given a choice: I could continue to descend into the darkness, or commit to moving into the light. It was as clear as that.

The life I had dreamed of when I was young was never going to be. All that anticipation had been a trap, and illness was trying to show me a way out. Where I had taken a wrong turn was in my belief that to honour my former self I needed to rail against what was happening to me. I needed to fight and kick and scream. I needed to push against the annihilation that I had believed was imminent.

But the only way to play this game was to accept the pathway that I'd been pushed along. And I began simply by asking the question – what will I do now? Not in desperation, but with the full-bodied hope that there would be something ahead for my future, if I jumped.

fourteen

a new life

I was home with a baby and an illness, which meant we were both regularly bursting into tears. There were days when I was so tired that I couldn't play with my daughter the way we both wanted, and as she grew, she would pull at my arms and try to get me up. But it was a wonderful life together. We moved around our neighbourhood, making friends and finding things to keep us occupied. I would tell her often that she had made me well, and that when I was pregnant she had filled me with her beautiful life. AJ had finally started his studio and found a space close to home, and was able to roll around with the two of us each day before and after his work. I felt I'd slowly worked it out. If I was alert, if I watched my illness carefully, I might be able to get ahead of it, and steer myself in a better direction. Because it wasn't illness that had destroyed my life so much as the fear it drew out of me.

When I finally realised this, something inside me shifted. That fear was far older than my illness — it went all the way back to when I was three years old, when my appendix was taken out, and it had been controlling me ever since. I hadn't been living even before I had become sick; I had been afraid to. I had taken the safe route. Teaching was something I wanted to do, but it certainly wasn't a risk. It hadn't pushed me out of my comfort zone. And there had always been a disquiet that made me scratch. I knew there was another life for me if I could only find a way through.

One moment kept coming back to me. I was lying in a hospital bed at some point during the past eight years of sickness, looking down to the park across the road. I watched as people walked through: some stopped and sat down with friends, some rushed along on their way to work. As I watched them secretly from above, I yearned to swap places with them, to be in those bodies walking through the park, to feel the lightness that I could detect from all the way up on the seventh floor. In that moment, in the simplicity of that desire, I realised that all the things I thought I'd lost were a mirage.

I'd made too much of living. I had complicated it. I had wrapped it in complexity and fear. I had endlessly wondered what would go wrong. I had expected the worst. Now that I'd been stripped of everything I'd thought I was, I had the chance to look at it all clearly. What had all that fear been *for* anyway? What mattered now? To be light and to feel the earth under my feet was all I really needed. To feel the silence and peace of a good, simple moment. It was all I wanted. It was the only thing left that I cared about. And if I couldn't walk through that park physically, at least I knew where I could locate that feeling inside me. I closed my eyes and travelled down to where it was, where those people in the park were, and I was filled with the same light, the same sense of discovery, the same deep love.

I had the chance to rebuild, but this time without the constant fear of collapse, because I'd collapsed before and I knew I could survive. I decided to rebuild my life in the way I should have been living it all along. After everything had been lost – my university studies, multiple jobs, my freedom, the future I'd planned – I had the opportunity for a whole new beginning.

For the people who knew me through that time, there was a noticeable shift in my behaviour. The anger was gone. It didn't make sense to me anymore. In the years that followed, I pursued everything that I had dreamed of when I was a child. I no longer had a fear of failure. It was as if I was running out of time.

One of those dreams had always been to work in radio. I had dabbled in it at university but I had never been brave enough to even consider how I might get into that kind of work; I didn't know where or how I would start. As a kid, I had loved to make my own radio shows, speaking into the in-built mic of our family's tape recorder. A thrill would run through me each time I simultaneously pressed the *Play* and *Record* buttons. I would first record myself as Prime Minister Bob Hawke answering a series of questions, then play that back on another tape player while I recorded myself asking the questions.

A decade later, at the start of my illness, I'd worked in a cafe on the rooftop of Triple R, one of the best community radio stations in the world. I would watch quietly as the presenters of my favourite shows – *Kinky Afro, The Australian Mood, Breakfasters* – came into the cafe, and I would try to look nonchalant as I made them coffee, or heated up rice balls. I would think about one day being brave enough to knock on the door of that radio station to see if there might be something, anything, that I could do. But I had never mustered the courage.

My good friend Talei, who I had worked with at the Rooftop Cafe, had made some friends in radio during that time and in 2006 was offered an opportunity to learn the ropes in the Triple R studio. She was a brilliant musician who had a great love of music, having grown up singing with her family. So she asked if I might be interested in joining her, for moral support. The moment I was behind the panel, I felt like I had come home. Phil, who had been working at Triple R for years by this stage and who had taken us under his wing, told me that I had 'that look' – he didn't explain it, but I think he meant the look that you get when you've found yourself exactly where you've always wanted to be. There is a beauty in the dance that you learn behind a radio panel, shifting faders and pressing buttons until they start to feel like extensions of your body.

It took some time, but eventually I was the volunteer presenter of a weekly local music show. It was the first time in a very long time that I felt like I belonged to a wider world and that I could do something that might be useful. I would listen to hundreds of music submissions every week. There was a special pigeonhole at Triple R that I would empty a couple of times a week, CDs tumbling out. I would take them home and listen to every single one, make notes and bring in the pick of them to play. Every time I walked through the front door to present that show, I was filled with excitement.

For so many years, I had found it nearly impossible to hold down a job. But I loved this, and was determined not to let my illness stop me. Soon a paid part-time job came up at the station that needed some local music insight, and after an arduous interview process, I can remember where I was when I got the call that told me I'd got the job. I was filled with the thrill of imagining myself back in a workplace and part of something again. It was the start of the happiest work I have ever done. But I had no idea if I could keep it together, if my illness would hold for long enough to get me to and from work. I told my managers as little as I could about the disease, the surgeries, the risks, and threw myself into the work.

***

It's sobering to think that the world is littered with chronically ill people who can't reliably pay their rent or their bills. Before I got sick, I'd volunteered with a food relief charity, which provided a dose of reality that I mostly tried hard to ignore. So many stories there began with someone becoming ill before their life fell to pieces.

One man, who I've thought about a lot over the years, had been living an entirely functional life, complete with a wife and children and a growing business. That was until he found himself with kidney disease. The need for dialysis to keep him alive meant that he slowly lost his capacity to hold the business together, and when the business failed, so did his marriage. By the time I met him, and was handing him tins of beans and a small amount of cash to see him through the next couple of days, he had lost it all. That same story was repeated over and over again by so many people I met through that charity.

But many of us forget that we are all hanging by a thread. We rely on being physically and mentally 'well enough' to consistently put in a day's work and earn a regular wage. If we are somehow rendered less capable and less reliable, the foundations of our lives can begin to crumble.

It is shocking to realise how very vulnerable we are. Far more comfortable to believe that difficult things happen to other people, and to assume that this man was lining up for baked beans because he'd somehow brought it upon himself. We can't bear the idea that we could easily be in that position, and the hostility that we often see played out toward people living on the fringes is surely connected to that fear.

But when chronic illness or disability is a reality, and work has suddenly become impossible, what options do we have? In Australia, there is a welfare system that many would rightly assume was built to assist people in this very situation. I spent several years — crucial, lifesaving time — getting a welfare payment in the form of the

Disability Support Pension (DSP). But it seemed to me as if the system had been built in the hopes most people would not have the resilience to wade through the endless appointments, the confusing and circular paperwork, and the piercing personal scrutiny.

Christine Walker, the CEO of Chronic Illness Alliance, has found that many people with chronic illnesses find it difficult to navigate the welfare system. In particular, having an invisible chronic illness means that you may appear healthy to welfare staff, particularly if your illness happens to be under control at that moment. As Christine says, 'a lot of chronic illnesses are actually episodic; [there are] long periods of time when people might be well, and other times when they virtually can't get out of bed. And that's completely underappreciated.'

Recent policy changes to the DSP have tightened the qualifying parameters even further, so that many people who should be supported – according to medical advice – are not. Now applicants need to satisfy a stringent test in the form of an 'impairment table' that scores them on various 'work-related impairments'. Many people with chronic illness are finding it difficult to prove, through this method, that they are unable to work.

One such person was Mandy Hunwick, who was diagnosed with multiple sclerosis (MS), along with autoimmune arthritis and vasculitis, a disease that restricts blood flow. When she went to apply for welfare support, she believed it would be a simple process of proving her condition and how it seriously impaired her ability to work. She had supporting documents from her health professionals – doctors with decades of experience – but she still encountered months and months of red tape and a series of rejections. She was required to prove to welfare staff who were not medically trained that she was not fit for work. As Mandy says:

"'You're not disabled enough. You haven't met all the requirements. You haven't supplied us with enough information. You haven't done this, you haven't done that. We don't think that you fit the bill, sorry, sorry, we don't accept this piece of paperwork, and you're going to have to appeal it." So I said, "All right, I'll appeal it and I'll supply some more information, which is what I did."'

The process of rejection and scrutiny can put an immense pressure on a situation that already feels like it is bearing down upon you.

'I struggled a lot mentally with ... [the] rejection from Centrelink. Because I really felt like, well if they can't support me financially and I can't get the assistance that I've been told I need and that I deserve, and I'm exhausted or sick all the time – like, I'm having surgeries for this – what the heck am I gonna do? ... How am I going to navigate this?'

And even for those like Mandy, who after eighteen months was one of the 'lucky' ones to receive a pension, that pressure does not abate. A big question mark has been placed over your claims to illness and incapacity, and so you might doubt whether you are indeed entitled to this 'kindness'.

When I was receiving the pension, there were days when I was well enough to get out and go to the shops or visit a friend and have a coffee. But I always did so wondering if there was someone from the department watching me. It was a feeling deep in my stomach that I was doing something wrong and might be caught out at any moment. I wondered if I would end up on one of those hostile current affairs programs that prey on a fear of 'welfare cheats'. Mainstream media has propagated an image of people receiving welfare as either bludger or rorters or both. Charged by a seemingly unquenchable desire to create a link between personal tax payments and welfare frauds, the media has marched dutifully to the drum of any government body hoping to improve its bottom line. In Australia, at least, this has been achieved. The number of people receiving the DSP peaked at 830,000 in 2014. By late 2018 that number had shrunk to 750,000. Public sentiment, coupled with a system that is difficult to navigate, has meant that many people who should be receiving a DSP are now on a lesser job-seeking payment, looking for work that they will likely be unable to maintain.

For me, this self-questioning played right into my insecurities about asking for and receiving help, and it was a self-questioning that still played on my mind as I tried to rebuild my life.

***

It had been five years since my ileostomy, and in that time no doctor had mentioned how long it might stay on, or if it would even be possible to reverse, and now, they had finally decided to broach the subject. As if I should have always expected it, they told me that it was time to think about the bag becoming permanent. The bag had allowed them to correct a lot of the damage of the fistulas, and had somewhat minimised the impact of the disease. I felt foolish that I had believed their early ruse about it coming off after a few months. One of my doctors conceded that not many people ever get it reversed. 'Of course,' I said, laughing with him, 'I wasn't stupid enough to believe it was a temporary thing.'

There were points throughout those years when they spoke of removing my entire rectum. 'Imagine that,' I would say when I told friends about it, widening my eyes. Then I would half-laugh and trail off. Imagine that indeed. I tried to figure this in my mind, to picture how this body that didn't feel like it belonged to me might be changed even further. Every time I tried, I would come up with a blank.

But not long before I started at Triple R, after much surgical repair and the hard work of doctors, it was agreed that we could work toward getting it reversed. The thought of having my body working the way it used to occupied my mind for days. I would spend hours imagining eating whatever I liked, swimming without fear, wearing tight jeans – and I allowed a small amount of hope to grow inside me.

But of course, it wasn't as simple as taking the bag off and finding myself transformed back into who I'd been five years before. The girl who went into that operation didn't exist anymore. I had connected to this new body in a way that I hadn't previously imagined possible. The ileostomy had made sure that I was anchored inside me, conscious not of how my body looked but of how it felt. And as much as I dearly wanted to remove the bag, it had somehow become part of me. I navigated the world through it. My identity had been mediated through it. I would have to learn myself again without it.

I remember being wheeled into the theatre that day, the same way I had been wheeled in when I first had the bag attached. Once again, I felt down to my stomach, where the bag was, and said goodbye. I ran my hands across the multiple scars that were there now, one that had allowed a baby to enter the world. Our baby. And one that reached right across my abdomen, which had been with me nearly my entire life. Soon there would be one more. And just as I had done years before, I felt the hurt of yet another transformation.

The weeks after it was removed were painful. It was frightening to wait for that part of my body to wake up again and be used after it had been asleep for so long. And I was filled with the anticipation of what this was going to mean. The removal of the bag brought to light how long my body had relied on a manual lever to fulfil its basic functions. With its removal came liberation from constantly thinking about the bag: the worry that it would break, the reliance on services to make sure I had enough stock at all times, the fear that I might eat too much and cause a blockage. Suddenly, I was free.

But the bag being removed also meant a return to the symptoms I'd lived with at the peak of my illness. I'd traded one type of enslavement for another.

My health and function deteriorated, but I didn't tell my work about any of it. I was too scared that they might get tired of my illness, and my potential unreliability. This sort of fear was unfounded, but nonetheless built into me: no one could be completely trusted. So even as my weight began to drop and my body visibly changed, I refused to miss a show. At times I became so sick that I didn't know how I was going to sit there for two hours and present the program. But I was so determined to keep my secret that I steeled myself, forcing myself to deal with the pain.

***

How well is the workforce equipped to deal with ongoing, incurable illness? The resounding answer is ... well, not well at all. The sheer size and variability of the workforce makes the enforcement of fair work policies extremely difficult. Discrimination against people who are chronically ill happens in covert ways that are difficult to prove, because it's so easy to find other explanations.

When I'd begun to creep back into the workforce, I'd known there would only be a small capacity for me to flip-flop between wellness and illness. I sensed that no matter how much your boss genuinely cared for you, the relationship was bound by realities beyond the personal. Ultimately, the relationship is fundamentally economic and is equated as such. As a worker the primary role is to be a functioning commodity. You are paid for; you must deliver a service. In Australia, you have no legal obligation to tell your employer about your illness, unless it directly impacts a specific aspect of the role – such as the ability to undertake physical tasks or sit for long periods of time. On top of that, your employer doesn't have the right to ask you questions about your illness, though of course this can be complex when work relationships so often straddle the personal and the professional. Just when is it right to share information about your illness, and how can you tell whether the sharing of that information will help or harm your position at work?

I met Silvi through our illnesses; she was making a podcast about chronic illness and asked me to be involved. While we were together, we got to talking about past jobs. She told me a story about a time when she worked at a fast-food restaurant while putting herself through university. Diagnosed with ulcerative colitis, she found herself experiencing a flare-up of her disease that required a short period of hospitalisation for some intravenous steroids. When she met with her employer to ask for sick leave, he was annoyed that she hadn't reported her illness at the time she got the job. Because she was unaware that it was her right not to disclose this information, she apologised, and upon further questioning, was asked to divulge more information about the nature of the illness, including the medication she was on. When she told him that she was on steroids, he winked at her and said, 'Is that the good stuff?' Her lack of awareness around her rights, coupled with her diminished power in a casual job that she needed to survive, meant that she didn't say anything.

When I first became sick I mostly worked for community organisations, so my utility was not always linked directly to income generation. Even so, there was always a very clear relationship between how efficient I was at my work and the money I was paid to do it. Showing up and doing 'an honest day's work for an honest day's pay' is a fairly universal concept across the workforce. The pervasiveness of this perceived link between honesty and working standard hours for a certain wage, means there is a perceived *dis* honesty in *not* working, in *not* getting a wage, in *not* fronting up to a workplace every day. And chronic illness does not play nicely with the consistent hours required for an 'honest day'.

It seemed right from the outset that my chronic illness, the one that might render me unable to work at any time, could not enter into the equation. If you come to work with a flu, or with a back that you've put out, the structure of the workplace supports you to resolve this issue and come back when it's all better. But there are no structures that meaningfully support an illness that is ongoing.

What I learned to do, very skilfully, was hide my symptoms. I developed strategies to deal with those symptoms. The vulnerability that I felt, and the concern that I could easily be replaced, propelled me to crawl out of bed and hide how hard it was to just be there at all.

I have spoken to many people who have found themselves in the same position. People who believed the only way they could stay in the world of the well and live a meaningful life was by hiding their symptoms and playing down the impact illness had on them. Some have hidden their illness to the extent that they would sneak off for hospital admissions without their employers knowing. You learn techniques to deal with your pain in public. You work hard to reframe your relationship with illness and you spend the weekend in bed, recovering and gathering yourself for the week ahead.

Esther Hannaford is a critically acclaimed musical theatre actress who recently played the lead role in multiple seasons of *Beautiful: The Carole King Musical* to sold-out crowds. What most didn't know, including other actors in her cast, was that her mostly controlled Crohn's disease worsened when the musical was set to open in a new city. 'I never wanted to say anything. Yeah, I was like, I've just got to prove myself, you know, and other people are taking days off for a cold, I'm at work every day, you know, I can barely function...'

She feared that if anyone knew the extent of her illness she would be replaced or it would destabilise the cast — or worse still, people watching her would be put off by knowing that she was sick:

'I think that surely everyone can see that I'm in a lot of pain in this moment, or something's happening. But I think you become very good at pretending ... I was in and out of the hospital getting on the drips and getting steroids just to get me through, and it was just a scary time. Because also if you haven't eaten, you don't have the energy or the mind space to navigate what is happening ... I guess I just felt really paranoid because I was really skinny. I felt very vulnerable and exposed because I couldn't hide that.'

***

Within the first couple of months of working at Triple R, I was in hospital again, and there was no avoiding people finding out. Triple R was the sort of community space that was more like an extension of your family. For better or worse, people drawn to this sort of place shared something vital: they cared about each other in the same way. So, as much as I wanted to keep it quiet, word spread. Since I hadn't had the time to really establish myself, I was worried that this would be what I would become known for. It was frightening to be so exposed to my workplace. What would happen if they decided that I was too risky to keep employed? No one wants to have someone at work who is unreliable, who is sick.

It brought about a strange kind of problem. I desperately wanted to work, and to claw back the years that I had missed out on building a career, but once my illness became known, well-meaning, caring colleagues would question the impact it might have on my health. I worried that my bosses would begin to make decisions on my behalf in the belief that certain kinds of work would be too much for me. It felt as though my sickness might become louder than my own voice. That I would be treated as the unreliable witness to my capacity.

I scoured the internet to try and find anything that would support my right to choose the type of work that I did, and to ensure that the 'duty of care' that might be applied to me by my employer wouldn't supersede my own right to choose how and when I worked. It was a strange form of discrimination that I hadn't expected to encounter. In fact, I hadn't expected my own ferocious determination to be back at work again. I hadn't accounted for the deep loss that I felt at being unable to build a working life.

But it wasn't only personal ambition that drove me. I was keenly aware of the divide that was growing between myself and people around me, who had worked consistently since leaving school or university. They were saving to buy houses. They were putting money in the bank for a rainy day. Now that I was up and walking again, I wasn't going to let anything get in my way. I hadn't been this person before I got sick. This steely vision, this work-at-all-costs attitude.

I was determined that illness would propel me into a new life. The decision that I'd made, when I decided to return to a world that was ultimately built for well people, was to hang in there at all costs. I was keenly aware that no one was going to stop to help me up. It was difficult to admit, but it's ultimately true.

From that point on, I was alert to what I might lose if my illness became too much of a focus for my managers and colleagues. I didn't trust that I would be seen as I wanted to be. I knew I might be thought of as unreliable, as someone who was annoying and sick. So, instead of letting everyone know when I was struggling, I chose one close work friend, Kate, and I would quietly go to her throughout the day and ask her to look at me with kind motherly eyes so that at least I could soften somewhere during my day. We would laugh at how absurd it was, but it genuinely gave me comfort, and it became a daily ritual. I worked hard to regulate my energy, to make my voice sound right, with no trace of strain.

Overall, though, I've been incredibly lucky. Every employer that I have worked for has cared about me as a person, and has shown compassion for how illness can make a life unpredictable. But so many workplaces are disabled by their own processes and their gross inability to enable a diverse workforce.

Before Mandy Hunwick sought support from the welfare system for her MS, she was employed by a government department in Australia – a department committed to rooting out transgressions on the part of its staff when it came to productivity, or the perception of productivity. When Mandy's illness started to worsen, she asked for changes to her role to accommodate it. She asked for hours that would work with her diminishing energy and increasing pain. Soon, after a long series of performance reviews that seemed set up to make her fail, she found herself almost at war with a management team who considered her illness no more than an excuse for inefficiency. She wasn't believed. Her treatment could almost be seen as comical if it didn't have such serious implications. After months of illness, she began to suspect that her employer was monitoring her.

> 'While I was having this issue of not being able to empty my bladder, I was going to the bathroom [a lot]. I obviously was very conscious of how often, so I would wait for as long as I possibly could. And because they were monitoring me so much, and some of my other colleagues, they would send one of the supervisors into the

bathrooms to monitor what we were doing. So obviously, I'd see her shoes come into the cubicle, hear her come into the cubicle. Over a few days, the number of times that she came in [while I was in the bathroom] was seventeen.'

When you are ill there always seems to be an assumption that you are trying to get away with something. Or that you are trying it on to get sympathy or support. It is up to you to bear the responsibility of proving that you are unwell. This is no more apparent than at work, where other people rely on you. They fear that others will need to work harder to support you. Even so, people have a patience for illness when there is a defined period, but when it has no boundaries, they can become hostile. Undermining your illness or your capacity to cope with it can become part of some of the more negative workplace rituals.

So how can we ensure that more people with chronic illness are capable of engaging in meaningful work? When we see our value only in what we make and what we do, in how 'busy' we are, we are lost. Of course, we know this. But as the pressures of life build up, we forget.

One of the greatest insights that chronic illness has afforded me, is the knowledge that when you are forced to stop and remove yourself from the everyday world, and lose the security that you will always be productive, you have a rare glimpse of what we know really matters. It is in the tiny details. It is the absence of the roles that you perform, the work you do, the function you play.

**

The beginning of my career in radio coincided with the beginning of my new life, a life where I found myself, not outside my illness, but directly inside. Right in the middle. It became clear that illness had not only transformed me, but my illness was who I was. It wasn't that I was subsumed by it, as I had been in previous years. Now, it was about knowing that it had impacted every inch of my being. It had rebuilt me and there was no way to know me now, without understanding the way that the illness was, in some ways, one of my greatest strengths.

It was in that first studio that I learned how to use my voice, to make the stream of air that travelled out of me so consistent that nobody could hear the wavering pain beneath it. I learned how to move the best parts of me into that stream, so the person my colleagues and listeners could hear, was the healthy me.

fifteen

a place in the system

Even though my ileostomy bag was gone, now and then I would feel a phantom wetness spreading across my leg and I'd have to feel the spot where the bag used to be to make sure it wasn't real. These moments always came with a shot of white panic. I had become so tense, so primed for a breakage, that it took a long time to realise I was safe – at least from that particular indignity.

But of course my old flare-ups were back – the fevers, the stabbing pain, the blood in the toilet, all coming and going. The chronic nature of this illness could not have been clearer. Whenever I thought I understood it, knew how to manage it, it would change shape on me.

The human mind doesn't really have the capacity to understand something 'chronic'. The idea of 'endless', of 'incurable', is a near impossibility. I had always imagined that when I had overcome a certain expression of this illness, whether it was the fevers, or the aches, or the fistulas, or the ileostomy bag, I would clock that level, like you do in a video game. I'd believed that I might acclimatise to each new symptom or treatment, leaving me strong enough to confront the next challenge – a slow but steady progression to 'better'. But the truth is, every relapse or new expression of an illness is a weight added to the one before.

But I was now truly coming to understand this illness, and that I needed to manage it as best I could.

***

Over the years, the ingredients in my daily cocktail of drugs went through many, many variations: when one therapy stopped working well, another drug or treatment or lifestyle change would be brought in to take its place.

Because each body will respond differently to any drug or treatment, a trial-and-error approach is necessary to find the best combination for each patient. For me, it felt as though my body was being put through a series of experiments. Each time the doctors would trial something new, it would take a couple of months before they could judge its efficacy. Then they would have to test out how the drugs worked in combination with other drugs. Nothing ever felt quite as effective as the first time I had been given relief, back when I was first diagnosed.

After many years of taking drugs daily, I started to fatigue. Suddenly, taking medication seemed to go against every instinct that I had. It wasn't exactly a choice – usually I would just get to the end of the day and realise that I hadn't taken them. But eventually, the very act of putting a pill in my mouth felt hard: I could feel them as they slid down my throat and made their way into my system. And I would feel a deep tug of depression, of hopelessness. I didn't know why. I had not had any disagreement with my doctors, and the act itself wasn't tiring as such, so why did I suddenly find it difficult?

It might have been an unconscious discomfort with the drugs and their side-effects, but to my conscious mind, it almost felt like self-sabotage. Why would I join the dreaded ranks of the 'nonadherent' when taking the medication could help to keep me out of hospital? I tried to research whether this happened to other people but couldn't find anything. I think that after years of taking drugs, a deep fatigue can grow within you. Medication was a reminder that I was fragile, reliant on this system and these companies. I'd had enough of that vulnerability.

One day, I was lying in bed, waiting out a painful flare-up, when my daughter, now three years old and bored, came up to me. 'I want you to get up,' she growled. 'Why don't you get better? Why don't you go to a doctor to get better?'

The frustration of the 'well world' was laid bare before me. Had my daughter hit on some unpleasant truth? Was I really not trying hard enough to get better? If I'd just taken the drugs like I was meant to, kept on top of all the tests and treatments, would I have been able to avoid this flare-up?

I felt tremendous guilt. I had wonderful doctors who tried to understand why I didn't follow the prescriptions as I should and would work with me on strategies to subvert my resistance. But it kept on happening. Every time I had an appointment, I would squirm in my chair and try to make the situation sound better than it was. I tried to make it seem like I wasn't rejecting their plan for me, and hoped that they'd believe me.

**

Complementary therapies, the incredibly wide and diverse array of them, can provide an important option for people seeking answers and remedies for their health. According to a study published in *Scientific Reports* in 2018, approximately 62 per cent of Australians have used complementary medicine, and for many it works. Where Western medicine is limited in its capacity to respond to some, if not all, symptoms of some conditions, alternative medicine has, in some instances, proven to be a salvation.

This was the case for Zoe, who I had spoken to about her struggle to get her diagnosis of myasthenia gravis. She found herself disagreeing with her neurologist over the medication they were prescribing and decided that the only way she was going to live well with her rare condition was if she took control of her health decisions:

> 'I remember crystal clear walking out of this neurologist appointment and being like, I need to be the CEO of my company now. I'm the only one who cares enough to make me better and I don't want to take the cancer drugs anymore because my hair is falling out. And so I did heaps of research and tried lots of stuff that they recommend for MS. And I started seeing a different nutritional doctor, and over the process of a couple more years, got off those cancer drugs.'

I was less inclined to go down that path. In some of the harder interactions I had with people, alternative and complementary therapies had often been suggested almost as an accusation. 'Have you tried acupuncture/ reiki/ yoga/ naturopathy/ sound therapy?' was often one of the first questions I was asked when I told someone that I was sick. Such was the scepticism of Western medicine that, for these people, unless I'd tried the alternative, I hadn't really tried to deal with my illness at all.

I had tried complementary and alternative therapies – partly from curiosity. At one point, I lay on a kinesiologist's massage table in a room made almost entirely of wood in the middle of a forest on the outskirts of Melbourne. She read my body through a series of taps and by holding my wrist, and told me that it was likely this illness had occurred due to the fright I got when I was three and my appendix ruptured. She may have been right, but I didn't go back to see if she could heal my fear. I drank concoctions of herbs made by a local Chinese medicine practitioner and gave up every food group, one by one, to see what difference that might make. At one point, I ate according to my blood type. I read a book by Louise Hay that suggested Crohn's disease was a result of an inferiority complex. Shiatsu, acupuncture, meditation, Flametree, naturopathy, hypnosis – you name it, I gave it a go. And none of it worked for me.

Then, one day, I learned that my hospital was running an eight-week intensive meditation course to help deal with chronic pain. So I went along. In that old hospital room, people who had never meditated before, who had never even imagined that they would ever meditate, found themselves lying on the worn carpet and breathing into their pain. It was a completely different approach for so many of us, to see our bodies as the source of the pain, but also as the solution. We were given a supported opportunity to challenge the concepts that we had about our own pain, and to find ways to reintegrate with our bodies, which had come to feel more like battlegrounds. And for a bunch of people who had never meditated before, we went in hard.

In those first sessions, when I was asked to focus on certain parts of my body, I just couldn't find them. I had been so determined to deny my physical experience that I had ignored it out of existence. It was a sobering thought.

The expectation was that we would meditate for at least an hour a day. It seemed outrageous, but I realised it's pretty incredible how you can find a spare hour if you really believe you should. So I surrendered to this process. I made detailed notes about how I was feeling both mentally and physically before I started, and I found that hour to meditate each day. The results for me, and for other members of the group, were nothing short of profound. I saw a marked decrease in my anxiety and a renewed connection to a body I had long practised to ignore. It wasn't an instant solution, but it was a moment of hope.

Perhaps I had more power over this illness than I'd thought.

***

One day I walked into my public hospital appointment, only to find that one of my favourite gastroenterologists had been replaced. I sat down uncomfortably in front of the new guy, Dr John Ding, who looked like he'd just graduated from high school. I was anxious to get it over with.

I began, as I always did, trying to explain why I hadn't been doing everything I should have done. My blood tests were late – sorry. I missed one of my injections – sorry about that. I hadn't been totally on top of my meds – sorry. I haven't been feeling very well, but that's probably my fault – so sorry for not doing everything that I should have.

Dr Ding stopped me mid-sentence and said, 'I really want you to know that I'm not judging you. We're here to help you. I'm totally on your side. In fact, I'm impressed with everything that you've been through. I'm impressed you're doing so well being a mum and working and being sick. We'll just work together and do the best we can.'

And I was speechless. In the entire time that I had been sick, I had never had anyone tell me that I had done a good job. What even was a good job? But it felt like he understood that to be managing my life while I was sick was enough to be proud of.

It sounds simple, but in that moment, an enormous weight lifted off my shoulders. After all the guilt and the shame that I had carried for having an illness, I actually felt for the first time that I was being truly understood.

John perfectly encapsulated something I'd been searching for, for years, though I'd never been able to put it into words: a balance between science and humanity.

Science measures our state of health or illness against a central mark, something we call 'normal'. This idea of a 'normal', functioning human body is essential for the sciences to communicate across time and disciplines. It's also essential in medicine's quest to return the human system to an agreed point so it can be understood as 'healthy'. But, I'd long begun to wonder if we'd adopted this approach at the peril of understanding illness's broader impact on the human being. The scientific approach to illness rarely captures the nuanced, individual experience of illness across the kaleidoscope of different personalities and chronic illnesses. Sickness is not one thing, but the medical system can make it feel like it is. I realised that across all my interactions with health care workers, good and bad, I'd longed to be seen not just as a body but as a person.

In her book *Bird's Eye View* Canadian health care advocate Sue Robbins explores how we might reshape the way we think about training professionals who work in health care. I caught up with her to discuss this balance that I suspected was missing from most approaches to illness:

> 'I think the best health care professionals are a combination of arts and science. So I think health care is actually an art, and what I fear is that we veered into too much science because, really, health care is about relationships between people. It is not just about the research or the data.'

While it makes sense to ask our health care workers to be both scientifically and emotionally developed, how do we go about achieving this?

I had an opportunity to speak with Dr John Ding himself about how he understood the role of empathy in dealing with his patients:

> 'Science is that harsh reality, and you have to then blend in that compassion where you're trying to distil the scientific, cold, hard fact down into the grey zones of individuals, where it's the patient that's

sitting in front of you, who has many other realities in their lives.

'And I just try to understand their points of view. Trying to communicate that science and blend it into a discourse between patient and doctor is the real challenge. But I see that as my responsibility, and taking patients along and seeing their context and actually finding a compromise or some sort of middle ground that you can build on from there.

'I think the starting point again for understanding patients is, of course, hearing their story, hearing where they've come from and what has led them to this point in their lives.'

I feel enormously grateful that John Ding is still my doctor in a public health system that struggles with consistency. The system I entered twenty-odd years ago has come a long way, but what I have understood throughout this experience is that there needs to be greater understanding of the complex impact that chronic illness has on the patient, so that every interaction acknowledges the experience of the individual.

John has been involved in his own research, which looks at how specialists regard the disabilities of their patients. He found that when the patient is well, the patient and doctor are usually in agreement about the health experience and the degree of disability that they are experiencing. But when the patient begins to struggle with their health condition, there is a marked divergence between how the patient and the doctor each measures the situation on the disability index. Doctors are far more likely to under-score the experience.

But does the pressure that health care professionals are put under in their graduating years mean that in reality there has not been enough support for them to improve their empathy? *The Australian Journal of General Practice* reported on the topic:

> 'Australian doctors have higher rates of stress and more attempts at suicide than the general Australian population, with an increased burden on those in their junior medical years and early stages of training. Burnout has been recognised as a causative factor for depression and suicide in the medical profession. It is considered to be a response to multiple significant stressors and incorporates feelings of emotional exhaustion, depersonalisation and reduced personal accomplishment.'

I was interested to hear from John about his experiences when he was a young doctor and how much pressure he was put under when he went through medical school:

'I think as doctors, the ones that I see progress the most are the ones that acknowledge their inadequacies or frailties and know they need to learn. I hadn't experienced a lot of failure in my life in terms of grades, so I got a big smack in the face when I failed the second part of the physician exam. That was a huge thing. I was twenty-three and everything was going swimmingly, and I thought the world was my oyster. It was emotionally distressing initially when I found out that I had failed and, you know, that only maybe one or two in my hospital hadn't passed. But eventually I think it's made me a better doctor; I think I'm a much better doctor actually having experienced failure and actually acknowledging that failure isn't the end of you, and it will only make you a better person. It sounds cliché, but it really strengthened that ability.'

John sought support to get through the devastation of having to wait another year before he could retake that physician's exam, and he found a language for his experience that has helped him with the complex terrain of caring for his patients:

'I don't think I had the vocabulary, and I think the growth comes in actually having the words to speak to patients who are outside of our scientific context. I never had that emotional vocabulary; I didn't actually have any of the tools that might engender one to want to talk more or discuss more about various aspects of their life.'

***

The care that has meant the most to me over the past twenty years has been in those simple acts of human kindness. Kindness that somehow emerged in what was usually a stark, clinical setting. And while the kindness that profoundly moved me was always something simple, such as the touch of a hand or a look that conveyed understanding, actually having the time and space and instinct to perform these small acts is not so simple. They require the time and capacity to look out beyond your own experience and touch into the experience of another. It takes a willingness to cross into someone else's life. To cross into the unknown and murky interior life of another human.

The words of my gastroenterologist years before kept coming back to me: 'Do you want your mechanic to be nice and laugh at your jokes, or do you want him to be a good mechanic?'

While we hope desperately to be seen as a complex human by the small team of people who provide our health care, usually we're just one of thousands that they will see over their careers. Inside the machine of the health care system, all I wanted was to be understood, and to find comfort. But maybe this was not achievable. Maybe expecting the person who has been charged with making us well to also understand us, comfort us, is unrealistic. But I've had enough good encounters with health care workers, even among the bad, to give me hope that this is not the case.

***

Between building a health care team that I trusted and feeling more confident about expressing what I needed, I began to creep towards a better way of managing my illness. I was learning how to work within the system, but also how to search outside of it when I needed. I still struggled to stay on top of all my treatments, and my ambivalence about drugs never really went away, but I'd managed to find a middle ground that felt right. I still see Dr Ding and my family even sees Dr Jeff, the GP who first helped me get diagnosed. In some ways, these relationships have been some of the most consistent and important in my life.

sixteen

seen

At a conference, Paralympian Karni Liddell once talked about that moment when a soon-to-be parent is asked about their hopes for their baby. The conversation will often start with the words 'What are you hoping for?' which is really just a covert enquiry about the parent's preference of gender, but the answer almost always deflects to a more palatable, 'I just want a healthy baby.'

What Karni realised, having been born with a muscle-wasting disease, was that she was the baby that parents were wishing they wouldn't get. It is hoped that we will be born 'normal'. What Karni Liddell took pains to point out is that illness, sickness and disability are statistically a fairly frequent occurrence, and therefore, by definition, *are* normal.

It is how evolutionary biologist Marlene Zuk understands illness in her book *Riddled with Life:*

> 'Life is naturally tattered, infested, bitten off, bitten into. The stem with a broken leaf, like an animal with lesions on its internal organs or less-than-glossy feathers, is more normal than its unscarred

counterpart. An unblemished animal – or person – is idealised and fictional, like the advertisements showing a solitary traveller at the Eiffel Tower. It doesn't really exist except in our imaginations. Disease is part and parcel of how we are supposed to look, of how we are supposed to live.'

There must be a better way to think about something so common, so normal, but twenty-five years on from when I first felt symptoms, I feel very little has changed in how we think about chronic illness. And part of the reason for that is how hidden these experiences are.

Chronic sickness starts as days and becomes months and then years. I am into the multiple decades now. It has been strange to look over the extent of my illness, from this position way in the future, and write about experiences that feel like they might have happened yesterday. So formative were they to who I am now, that for a time it felt strange that new friends or new close colleagues would not realise I'd had these experiences, would not even know I was sick. It felt like without this part of my story, I was only partially known.

The intervening years have been very much like the beginning of this story: wild peaks and troughs that made me feel like an observer of my own life, as I've ultimately been incapable of influencing the way the illness behaves. But in the past couple of years, I have finally found medication that has worked well – enough for me to begin to feel the regular beat of a life that is not dominated by illness. It has shifted me out of the grey, and I finally feel that, if I were asked, I could honestly answer that I am well. But it doesn't shake the knowledge that this may change at any moment. I am still captive.

The quiet ferocity with which I began working again after that long period of illness, didn't abate. After some wonderful years at Triple R, it was time for me to move on and, after flying loose in the wind for some time, I applied for a job at the ABC, working as the music director for their local radio network. I was utterly shocked when I got the job, but the next couple of years were some of the happiest of my working life. I worked hard, really hard. Yes I loved the work, but I had also lost almost ten years of my career to illness, and the hunger to catch up drove me. I came to understand, in my small way, how the world outside our sick bodies is not built to accommodate health differences – you either keep up, or you're out. And so I mostly denied the experience of my ill health. I worked through unbelievable pain in order not to fall back further than I already had.

I'm not proud of this. It was pure, desperate survival, which is not how it should be for us. But in so many workplaces, denying your illness and hiding it from all those around you is the only way to survive. I still have no faith that our systems are built to cater for the chronically ill, and that vulnerability frightens me.

The systemic barriers that prevent more people with chronic illness from participating in satisfying work remain in place. It wasn't until the lockdown in response to the COVID-19 pandemic that businesses and organisations realised there are more ways to work than from nine to five, monitored by your boss in an office. Workplaces were moved online, giving employees freedom to work from an external environment. The idea that people could be trusted to do the work they were being paid for started to slowly ripple out. And for people with chronic illness, who could now negotiate a new way to work under the cover of a nationwide intervention, this revelation was well overdue.

All these years on from that moment when I was diagnosed, I finally decided to write this book because life for people with invisible chronic illness hasn't really changed. During the pandemic, the vulnerability of disabled and chronically sick people was made clear, as well as how little access to power these groups have. I am still afraid to tell the world outside my skin what is really happening inside me, and I know, from all the chronically sick people I've spoken to over the years, that I'm not alone in my hiding. So it became clear that I needed to add my voice to the calls for change.

We must find a way to speak about the experience of being chronically ill, a way that show the strength and unwavering fortitude of so many who live this kind of life. We need to see illness in the vastly diverse ways that it impacts us: how we are challenged by it, and how we are transformed by it.

***

'I guess no concessions for you? We only have a concession available for people with disability.' The cashier at the zoo smiled politely, then she saw my expression. I must have looked like I felt. I was embarrassed.

'Well, actually, I do have a disability concession...' I mumbled as I opened my wallet and pulled out the card. She turned white and scanned the concession that I handed to her.

'It's just that ... I'm sorry, I shouldn't have said that. I just thought it wasn't obvious.'

I didn't know what to say to her. I was embarrassed to be claiming something that she obviously assumed I didn't have a right to.

But she did what most people do – she looked at my appearance to assess if I had a disability. I guess I couldn't blame her; this was how most people thought about disability and illness. If it's real enough, surely you can see it? I almost gave her a full and thorough explanation about what was wrong with me. I almost needed to hear it myself, because I too felt uncomfortable claiming any sort of special consideration.

When an illness is largely unseen, the way you are automatically identified by others can make any decision to assert your own identity quite complex. It can feel like you are constantly trying to correct the record. I've been grappling with my identity as an ill person for years, and I still haven't quite made sense of it.

Many people who encounter barriers as a result of chronic illness, understand those barriers are often in place due to the social structures that privilege healthy, abled-bodied people. It is experienced in the way we need to navigate the world so we can get around, the way we work, or the way we simply cannot work because of physical constraints. When what you experience is invisible, the extension is that maybe your expression of it should be too.

There are enormous, complex and varied difficulties encountered by those who have illness and disability, and activists are doing incredible work in hostile environments to highlight these inequities. The issues encountered by those whose disabilities are invisible run alongside those of the visibly ill, often overlapping; sometimes diverging into distinct concerns and challenges. Asking for assistance, or in my case, a concession, when you don't 'look' like you should be receiving one can feel like an endless battle for recognition and support. You get caught in a loop of wanting to prove that you are ill while hoping you won't be unfairly limited by that illness.

So what can we do? Exactly how should we prove our illness to the world? In this case, I had a card that I could pull out to prove my status, but not everyone has this kind of proof, and even then it has limited applicability – a card won't get you a flexible job, or a quicker diagnosis, or more understanding from friends and family.

We must find a way to be seen. The experience of chronic illness needs to be understood broadly as more than basic 'sickness'. There remains a need to claim a legitimate space and identity for people who have invisible chronic illnesses, one that acknowledges the fundamental shared experiences and challenges that we face in navigating a world built for the healthy.

Without a clearly defined space for chronic illness, it is impossible to make the systemic changes we need.

For decades, cultural critics, academics and disability advocates have been searching for a better way to talk and think about disability and chronic illness. Many have rejected the distancing or 'othering' of disability identity, believing that disability can be empowered and should be understood as such an essential aspect of a person's identity that it is not 'experienced' so much as innate to the individual and their identity.

Carly Findlay, a renowned disability advocate, and editor, speaker and author of multiple books and articles on disability including *Growing Up Disabled in Australia* and her own memoir, *Say Hello,* explores her identity as formed by her experience with the rare skin condition ichthyosis. In 2017, she took to social media to articulate her own relationship with disability:

> 'Please don't erase my identity by telling me not to call myself disabled. Disability and being disabled is not a bad thing. When you use euphemisms like "differently abled", "special needs" or "additional needs" you're increasing the stigma around disability. For me, there's pride and culture in disability. "Disability" is a factual word, not an insult

or derogatory towards me and other disabled people.'

The reactions to this post diverged wildly – not everyone felt the same way – but what was clear was that this divergence of opinion itself needed to be acknowledged, and that identity cannot be assumed. It is complex.

What most disability advocates can agree on is that some of their greatest challenges with disability are caused by the systemic discrimination of a society that has long held low expectations of people with disability. Because of this, Stella Young, a disability advocate, helped promote the theory of the 'Social Model of Disability', which places the responsibility for the perception and treatment of disability 'as deficit' at the feet of broader society.

The Australian Federation of Disability Organisations explains:

> 'The social model of disability says that people are disabled by barriers in society, such as buildings not having a ramp or accessible toilets, or people's attitudes, like assuming people with disability can't do certain things. The medical model of disability says people are disabled by their impairments or differences, and looks at what is "wrong" with the person, not what the person needs. We believe that the

medical model of disability creates low expectations and leads to people losing independence, choice and control in their lives.'

An empowered disability identity forces society to recognise that not everyone can or wants to navigate the world in the same way, and that abled-bodied experiences and frameworks that support only the abled experience, are not the only legitimate ones. Equally, disability advocacy is constantly fighting for legislative support to ensure the end to discrimination that is rife through the layers of our system.

Individuals are often not one thing and have compounding and complex intersections with disease and disability. As the World Health Organisation defines, 'Disabilities is an umbrella term, covering impairments, activity limitations, and participation restrictions. An impairment is a problem in body function or structure; an activity limitation is a difficulty encountered by an individual in executing a task or action; while a participation restriction is a problem experienced by an individual in involvement in life situations. Thus disability is a complex phenomenon, reflecting an interaction between features of a person's body and features of the society in which he or she lives.

It feels important that we confront some serious questions around why society has such a hostile reaction to illness. Is there a sense that sick people are angling for sympathy or an easier ride? Perhaps there is a fear of being obliged to offer some kind of support? The scepticism chronically ill people encounter is usually covert but clear: *Why are you special? Why are you the one asking for compassion when I have suffered too?* We have such a visceral reaction to anyone we feel is not coping with their lot. 'Suck it up' is the refrain.

There is also a heroism ascribed to those who display resilience during illness. If you bear it without complaint, or you are seen to be fighting it and moving forward, or indeed if you have beaten your illness in some visible way, society is often more prepared to celebrate with you and, within that context, to recognise what you've been through. But what if your illness doesn't end in a party? What if it has an endlessness that doesn't allow for a cake? How can we celebrate the eternity of this experience?

In my case, with few options being offered by the outside world, the change had to start inside. I had to scrape away the layers of self-hatred, disgust and shame. Through many days spent in bed, through hospital admissions and waiting rooms, I had to totally reframe my understanding of illness. Eventually, I understood that being sick had given me a whole range of positive experiences that were otherwise largely inaccessible. I turned my understanding of illness upside down.

When asked, I have always said that I would never choose to not have this illness, or to have done this differently. I am proud of what the experience of illness has been in my life. Chronic illness is who I am.

***

When my daughter was eight years old, we had another baby. This pregnancy was a surprise, especially as it followed a miscarriage, and it felt much as it had that first time: as though some magical force had intervened to make the impossible real.

Partway through my pregnancy, what began as itchy hands turned into a liver condition called cholestasis of pregnancy. It continued to worsen, but a fortunate exchange with my doctor, who had seen it once before, picked up that the medication I was taking for my Crohn's disease might be causing it. For months before the birth I was in hospital every day, being monitored. The fear that I had learned to manage reignited. There was a real possibility that my child could die, and all that knowledge of human frailty –

the fact we are hanging by a thread, the fear that I thought I had finally eradicated – was really just sitting there, waiting to come back. And it blossomed and grew. I completely shut down, scared to make a noise. I travelled inside and hid there, counting the hours, the days, the weeks as my baby grew inside me. Hoping that if I was quiet enough, the darkness wouldn't find me.

This time, I didn't have to manage an ileostomy bag, but the scarring all over my abdomen had caused my insides to adhere to the abdominal wall, which meant that the birth was going to be risky. I remember hating the man who cut me open that day. As he peeked over the curtain to tell me that I wouldn't ever be able to have any more children because they had just missed cutting my bowel by the smallest of margins, I focused all my terror on him. For him it was just another day at the office, letting a woman know that she wouldn't be able to have any more children. And that she was lucky.

Lucky? Was I? Just as my dad had been all those years ago? Somehow this didn't feel lucky. It felt devastating. Scraping through by the skin of my teeth didn't feel like a victory.

And when they pulled out a beautiful little boy and laid him on my chest, like that first time when I held his sister, I felt an explosion of anguish. Just like with her, the fear of their death consumed every inch of me, and it took weeks for me to come back. I remember looking out the window of the hospital and not recognising anything anymore. The street below, which I had travelled up and down for decades, was no longer familiar.

***

The first time I ever spoke publicly about my illness was in an interview on a radio show at ABC Melbourne, where I now present the afternoon show. This was years after the firestorm had hit, and when I had found a way to explain it as truthfully as had slowly become possible.

The interview was conducted by my good friend and colleague, broadcaster Hilary Harper, who had also been through her own trauma having experienced multiple heart-wrenching miscarriages and the stillbirths of two babies, Arthur and Edwyn. The interview came about as a result of us reaching out to each other at work in an unguarded moment, when we found a space for us to explore some of the complexities of our bodies. We had both battled with the insecurity and danger that our bodies had caused, and were still grieving. Her interview opened me up, and together we found the words to talk about illness in a way that helped to shift some of the pain that had been lodged in me.

We talked about what it was like to live with a body that let you down, and about the pain of realising that your body isn't going to do what you had hoped and how it changed the dreams you could have for your life. I told the intimate parts of the story. And for one of the first times, I spoke about it as openly as if I were whispering it to myself.

The interview was pre-recorded, and the night before it aired, I rolled around in bed, wide awake and in a sweat. Why had I revealed myself this way? Why had I abandoned my resolve to remain secretive? Would people think I was disgusting? Would they judge me, mock me? Would they think I was complaining? More than anything, my fear of exposure revealed that I had not exorcised my self-disgust and shame.

My illness had been a decades-long struggle between the world outside and the truth that lived inside. More than finding it easier to hide my illness, I still felt like I was *expected* to. Being sick all the time is perceived as a real drag: the endless parade of apologies for falling short of the expectations. *Why didn't you come to the party? Why were you late for work? Why are you still in bed?* You are constantly confronted with the way you've let people down or missed opportunities that you might, in a past life, have grasped with both hands.

Sharing all this, telling the absolute truth, made me worry that I would be judged. I imagined my workmates being repulsed by me. I wondered how we might behave when we saw each other in the kitchen.

I was in the car with my family when it aired, and as soon as it was announced I held my breath. I realised my secrecy hadn't entirely been about shame, and how much I wanted to hide myself – it was also about how precious and intimate this experience was. My illness had forced a long, painful revelation of my inner world, and I was scared that if I shared it, these precious parts of me would be misunderstood or dismissed.

This book is partly inspired by that moment, and by a deep yearning to understand and break the silence at the centre of illness. It has been an attempt to find words that touch on the truth of this experience – the transformation, the annihilation, the wonder, the pain, the life, the death. I've tried to see it from every angle, beyond the limiting words that make up a diagnosis.

That day in the car, my kids were in the back, hearing me on the radio describe a time of my life that they understood only parts of.

As I sat in the front passenger seat beside AJ, I began to cry, and we reached out for each other, a years-long part of our story suddenly set free. Our children, whose lives had relied on my broken body, were tucked up safely in the back seat. We had travelled such an enormously long way just to sit in the beauty of that mundane scene: a family driving down the road.

acknowledgements

I acknowledge the traditional owners and custodians of the land on which I wrote this book, the land of the Kulin Nation. I acknowledge that sovereignty has never been ceded – it always was and always will be, Aboriginal land.

I may never write another book, so bear with me.

There are so many people who I need to thank for their support of this book, but also for their support of the life that I have captured within its pages.

The book first. As I mentioned, I never thought I would write this book, but slowly a seed found its way to germinate thanks to the loving tending of so many. Firstly, it took a little bit of serendipity for two old friends, who had held me through some of those early years of illness, to find their way into our orbit and tell me it was something I should do. A huge thank you for getting this ball rolling, Selin Yaman and Kalya Ryan.

I had no idea how I might write something like this until I gave a tear-drenched talk in front of a room of fellow Crohn's and colitis patients. Thanks to a beautiful ABC colleague, Kim Bassett, who escorted me there that day and gave me confidence to write some more. Thanks to Wendy Tuohy who was also a wonderful early support.

To the very wise and wonderful Violet, who has supported me for a decade or more in every minute aspect of my life. She knew that I would write this book and has encouraged and guided me – Violet, you are an utter gem.

To Monica 'whatever happened to us' Dux, a brilliant writer in her own right, who not only invited me to her writers' group – where I awkwardly spoke about my then half-baked book idea to some of the smartest women in town (thanks for your kindness Anne Manne, Christine Kenneally and Louise Swinn) – but also proceeded to knock on doors for me. And like a perfect stage mum, she gave me enthusiastic thumbs up, advice, hilarious anecdotes, wise counsel, and a night of romance with a dozen oysters (sorry, make that four). A bloody good sheila she is.

To Fiona Pepper who used her razor sharp skills to assist with the research of this book. Her insight and care has given this work its needed depth. She is also my great friend and walking pal and therefore required not only to be book smart but also to have a tremendous tolerance for witnessing every detail of this book and my life.

To other wonderful writers who are smart about life and who are eternally supportive of people like me who are venturing into this world for the first time – Nova Weetman, Peggy Frew, Clare Bowditch, Carly Findlay and Sami Shah (who told me I'm going to need a psychiatrist in eight months – true?). And a thank you to Carly Findlay who also read this book and offered her wise insights into the many facets of disability and chronic illness. To Clare Forster who was also very supportive at the beginning and gracious and warm in all our dealings.

To a couple of legends who took me off the mean streets and brushed my hair. A gal couldn't hope to have more dedicated, funny people on her side – thanks Lena Barridge and Henrie Stride for backing me right from the beginning of this book. And to Lena for getting me drunk when I should have been writing. A huge amount of love to you for being one of the very early readers, in fact, the earliest. Thank you for your brains and your face (that really doesn't look mean). I treasure how much I could trust you with the very precious stuff right at the start and for how much you've got my back.

To my work family who supported me by making sure the plates didn't break, especially

John Standish and Barbara Heggen. To the wonderful Dina Rosendorff, Warwick Tiernan, Kon Karamountzos and Sally Moore, who have given me the support and encouragement to get it done and get it out there.

To Sandy and Tim, who are outrageously generous and have invited me into their beautiful house many times to stay when I've needed to, including to write this book. And to Paula Thomson, who is never far away when many of the good things happen in my life – coincidence?

To the incredible health support that I have received over the years: so many nurses, doctors and health workers who have been instrumental in my life. A huge and specific thanks to Dr John Ding, Dr Jeff Wilcox, Dr Catherine Lazaroo, Dr Steven Brown and all the IBD staff (Tami and Steph) at St Vincent's Hospital in Melbourne. An especially big thank you to Dr John Ding for his generosity with his time and insight. John spent hours speaking with me about some of the ideas that I grappled with in this book. I feel very grateful for your care and for our conversations.

The biggest and warmest thanks to everyone I spoke to about their own experience of invisible chronic illness. I cannot thank you enough for the trust you gave me to hear your story. Your stories are tremendously moving and gave me a greater understanding of the extent and diversity of the experience of invisible chronic illness. I have done my best to honour your words and know that your stories will mean so much to others who find their way to reading this book. HUGE gratitude to Scarlett, Zoe, Rose, Graeme, Esther, Sherri, Rebecca, Collette, Mandy, Christine, Silvi, Gayle and Olivia. And thank you to Hilary Harper for your friendship and for helping me tell this story.

Thank you Sophie Michalitsianos for gifting me your beautiful words for the epigraph in this book.

And to the wonderful humans at Affirm Press. Thank goodness a shady international bit-coin crime ring didn't ultimately get in the way of this perfect marriage. Thanks Martin Hughes – you are simply the best. Thank you for trusting me and for being someone that I could trust. And Ruby Ashby-Orr, what a gal, what a master editor you are. Thank you for transforming my jumble of words into something that I am proud of. To all at Affirm, it was truly joyful.

And now to my life. This is primarily a story about invisible illness but to tell that story I had to share mine. And in sharing my story, I am sharing the story of many other people and the many beautiful family and friends who have been a significant part of mine.

Firstly to my family: thank you to AJ who has shared this story with me in every possible way and for his generosity in supporting my experience of this story to be shared here. He has played an enormous role in every minute of my life as a partner, a parent, a carer and a friend. He is not featured as extensively as is true to this story, but you can be sure he is written in between every line.

Thank you to my mum and dad, Anne and Pat, who held me when I was broken and who would do anything for me or any of their kids. Thank you for the refuge you provided me in those darkest days and for being at the end of the phone when I was most frightened. A huge thank you also to my excellent brothers and sister, Dominic, Matthew and Clare (and all their beautiful partners), for everything you have done for me. And to Bubba Smith, a wonderful M.I.L who supported both AJ and me through many years of illness, and our lives. And to Ken and Rosemarie, and all my extended family – thanks for welcoming me into your lives.

To a huge list of friends and work colleagues without whom I would not be here in quite the same way. This crew has been involved in hours of listening and visiting and supporting. Thank you deeply to my friend of thirty years, Ineke Hutter: you and Jocelyn and Theo were there through the hardest times and continue to be there always, I'm eternally grateful. Thank you Romy and Talei for your friendship. Thank you to Kate Blanchfield (and team) who always has my back and has always felt my brow in times of fever: your friendship has been treasured. And to Lauren Taylor for sharing conversations with me that I can rarely have with anyone else. To my Morries – Libby Chow and Kirsty Argyle for your eternal kindness and support and for our endless Tuesdays together. To Meg Stuart for showing me how to love words. And to my beauties Donna Morabito and Ainslie Hodgkinson, for helping me early on and always.

And finally to the Lolo Brothers and Co., AJ, Mika and Perry: you have all been with me at the crossroads I have encountered. We have travelled in and out of The Nothingness together. Our love is eternal. Thank you for everything you all are. Words are never sufficient to explain what you mean to me. Thank you for supporting me to get this book done, and the support and love you have given me to follow my heart-but mostly for the beautiful part you all play in my life. I am very grateful.

references

Introduction

'According to the Australian Institute of Health and Welfare, approximately 50 per cent of the Australian population reports having a chronic illness.'

Australian Institute of Health and Welfare, 2020. *Chronic pain in Australia*, AIHW, Canberra.

Chapter 1

'when individuals experience a major change (e.g. in health state), their internal standards, their values or their conceptualisation of quality of life can alter with it.'

Rees, J., O'boyle, C. and Macdonagh, R., 2001. 'Quality of Life: Impact of Chronic Illness on the Partner'. *Journal of the Royal Society of Medicine*, 94(11), pp.563–566.

Chapter 2

'People often posit the existence of supernatural "forces" or "spirits" to explain events'

Bastian, B. et al., 2019. 'Explaining illness with evil: pathogen prevalence fosters moral vitalism'.

Proceedings of the Royal Society B: Biological Sciences, 286(1914), pp.1576.

In the early 1950s, one of the founding fathers of American sociology, Talcott Parsons, described illness as a deviance as he developed a theory called the 'Sick Role'.

Faris, E. and Parsons, T., 1953. 'The Social System'. *American Sociological Review*, 18(1), pp.103.

Chapter 3

'It's not just your medical history your GP will be tracking either.'
Australian Medical Association, 2020. *Importance of A Trusted Regular GP Emphasised*. [online] Available at: ama.com.au/gp-network-news/importance-trusted-regular-gp-emphasised.

Gabrielle Jackson details the enormous historical backdrop for delayed diagnosis and misdiagnosis of women
Jackson, G., 2019. *Pain and Prejudice*, Allen & Unwin.

'The tendency to attribute women's physical complaints to mental illness has its roots in the history of "hysteria"'
Dusenbery, M., 2018. *Everybody Was Telling Me There Was Nothing Wrong*. [online] BBC.co

m. Available at: www.bbc.com/future/article/20180523-how-gender-bias-affects-your-healthcare.

'On some level, pelvic pain has been believed for centuries to be the deserved consequence of presumed depravity on the woman's part'

Nezhat, C., Nezhat, F. and Nezhat, C., 2012. 'Endometriosis: ancient disease, ancient treatments'. *Fertility and Sterility,* 98(6), pp. S1–S62.

'...this whole concept of somatisation would fall apart, and rapidly, if we started believing women.'

Wright, F., 2019. 'This Woman Is Hysterical', *Meanjin,* [online] Available at: meanjin.com.au/essaysthis-woman-is-hysterical/.

the great disparity at the coalface of medical research ... an 'over-reliance on male data' when it comes to both animal and human medical research'

Criado-Perez, C., 2019. 'End medical gender bias'. *New Scientist,* 242(3234), pp.23.

80 per cent of the healthcare workforce, but they only make up between 3 and 9 per cent (depending on the role) of leadership positions As written in

Lanka, V., 2019. 'How the health care leadership gender imbalance hurts your ogranisation – and four ways to make a change' [online] Available at www.advisory.com.

all is not equal in the Australian health system.

Australian Institute of Health and Welfare, 2018, *Australia's health 2018: in brief*, AIHW, Canberra.

delayed diagnosis can be attributed to the 'attitudes and behaviours' of healthcare providers

Hall, W., Chapman, M., Lee, K., Merino, Y., Thomas, T., Payne, B., Eng, E., Day, S. and Coyne-Beasley, T., 2015. 'Implicit Racial/Ethnic Bias Among Health Care Professionals and Its Influence on Health Care Outcomes: A Systematic Review'. *American Journal of Public Health*, 105(12), pp.2588–2588.

The best data we have in Australia is there are 30 per cent fewer procedures for Aboriginal patients across the country compared to non-Indigenous patients.

Humanrights.gov.au, 2020. *Achieving Aboriginal and Torres Strait Islander Health Equality Within A Generation – A Human Rights Based Approach|Australian Human Rights Commission.* [online] Available at: humanrights.gov.au/our-work/publications/achieving-aboriginal-and-torres-strait-islander-health-equality-within.

Zhou, N., 'Indigenous patients suffer racial bias in hospitals, Naomi Williams inquest told'. [online] Available at: www.theguardian.com/austr

alia-news/2019/mar/14/indigenous-patients-suffer-racial-bias-in-hospitals-naomi-williams-inquest-told.

Dr G Yunupingu was left to wait in a hospital for eight hours without treatment after presenting with complications to his hepatitis B

SBS News, 2020. *Darwin Hospital Accused of Racial Profiling In Gurrumul Yunupingu Treatment.* [online] Available at: www.sbs.com.au/news/darwin-hospital-accused-of-racial-profiling-in-gurrumul-yunupingu-treatment.

Indigenous Australians suffer a 2.3 times greater rate of burden of disease than non-Indigenous Australians

Australian Institute of Health and Welfare, 2016, *Australian Burden of Disease Study: impact and causes of illness and death in Aboriginal and Torres Strait Islander people 2011,* AIHW, Canberra. Available at: www.aihw.gov.au/reports/indigenous-australians/contribution-of-chronic-disease-to-the-gap-in-mort/contents/table-of-contents.

Having a rare disease, if we consider rarity as the defining characteristic, is another of the many reasons that diagnosis can be delayed.

Rare Disease Day, 2020. *Rare Disease Day 2021–28 Feb–Article.* [online] Available at: www.rarediseaseday.org/article/what-is-a-rare-disease.

'obtaining a diagnosis for their disease took a long time (more than five years)...'

Molster, C., Urwin, D., Di Pietro, L., Fookes, M., Petrie, D., van der Laan, S., & Dawkins, H., 2016. 'Survey of healthcare experiences of Australian adults living with rare diseases'. *Orphanet Journal of Rare Diseases*, 11, 30. doi.org/10.1186/s13023-016-0409-z.

'describes how adults who have not received a diagnosis often feel that they need to continually legitimise their illness to doctors'

Spillmann, R., McConkie-Rosell, A., Pena, L., Jiang, Y., Schoch, K., Walley, N., Sanders, C., Sullivan, J., Hooper, S. and Shashi, V., 2017. 'A window into living with an undiagnosed disease: illness narratives from the Undiagnosed Diseases Network'. *Orphanet Journal of Rare Diseases*, 12(1).

to regain some control, patients turn to 'Dr Google'

Murphy, M., 2020. *Dr Google Will See You Now: Search Giant Wants to Cash in On Your Medical Queries.* [online] *The Telegraph.* Available at: www.telegraph.co.uk/technology/2019/03/10/google-sifting-one-billion-health-questions-day/.

how and when people were using search engines to assess their health

Pennmedicine.org, 2020. *Health-Related Google Searches Doubled in The Week Before Patients' Emergency Department Visits – PR News.* [online] Available at: www.pennmedicine.org/news/news-r

eleases/2019/february/health-related-google-search es-doubled-in-the-week-before-patients-emergency-department-visits.

SBS News, 2020. *Paging Dr Google.* [online] Available at: www.sbs.com.au/topics/voices/health/article/2016/05/23/paging-dr-google.

Chapter 5

'many consumers have told us they are afraid to admit they live with a chronic pain condition'
Painaustralia.org.au, 2020. [online] Available at: www.painaustralia.org.au/static/uploads/files/mr-talking-about-pain-19072019-wflinylxybzd.pdf.

'the number of Australians who died from unintentional overdoses has increased by almost 38 per cent in ten years'
NewsGP, 2020. *Australia's Overdose Crisis Is 'Getting Worse'.* [online] Available at: www1.racgp.org.au/newsgp/clinical/australia-s-overdose-crisis-is-getting-worse.

'...the stress of coping with pain coupled with the increased likelihood of taking addictive drugs both compound the vulnerability to addiction.'
Mentalhelp.net, 2020. *Managing A Chronic Illness When You're Addicted to Prescription Drugs.* [online] Available at: www.mentalhelp.net/addiction/recovery/managing-a-chronic-illness-when-youre-addicted-to-prescription-drugs.

'In 2019, the total revenue of Australian Pharmaceuticals Industries Limited (API)...'

Hinton, T., 2020. 'Revenue of Australian Pharmaceutical Industries Limited in Australia from 2015 to 2019'. Available at: www.statista.com/statistics/1062361/australia-revenue-australian-pharmaceutical-industries-limited/.

'We located an abundance of consistent evidence demonstrating that the industry has created means to intervene in all steps of the processes'

Stamatakis, E., Weiler, R., & Ioannidis, J.P., 2013. 'Undue industry influences that distort healthcare research, strategy, expenditure and practice: a review'. *European journal of clinical investigation*, 43 (5), 469–475. doi.org/10.1111/eci.12074.

'Patients may need to purchase food instead of hypertensive medication,'

Scarlett, W. and Young, S., 2016. 'Medical Noncompliance: The Most Ignored National Epidemic'. *The Journal of the American Osteopathic Association*, 116(8), pp.554.

'"Noncompliant" is doctor-shorthand for patients who don't take their medications or follow medical recommendations.'

Ofri, D., 2020. *When the Patient Is "Noncompliant" – Danielle Ofri*. [online] Available at: danielleofri.com/when-the-patient-is-noncompliant/.

Chapter 6

'The only thing you can count on is the fact that you never really know what your day is going to look like'

Trunzo, J., 2020. *It Takes Psychological Flexibility to Thrive with Chronic Illness – Joseph Trunzo | Aeon Essays*. [online] Available at: aeon.co/essays/it-takes-psychological-flexibility-to-thrive-with-chronic-illness [Accessed 13 July 2020].

called this 'engulfment'

Van Bulck, L., Luyckx, K., Goossens, E., Oris, L. and Moons, P., 2018. Illness identity: Capturing the influence of illness on the person's sense of self. *European Journal of Cardiovascular Nursing*, 18(1), pp.4–6.

Chapter 7

'is care that is respectful of, and responsive to, the preferences, needs and values of the individual patient'

Safetyandquality.gov.au, 2020. *Person-Centred Care | Australian Commission on Safety and Quality In Health Care*. [online] Available at: www.safetyandquality.gov.au/our-work/partnering-consumers/person-centred-care#:~:text=Person%2Dcentred

%20care%20is%20widely,values%20of%20the%20individual%20patient.

Chapter 8

Given the strength of the cultural rules about physical contact present in even a seemingly relaxed Western culture, it might be expected that students learning physical examination techniques would find performing physical examination

Dabson, A.M., Magin, P.J., Heading, G. et al., 2014. Medical students' experiences learning intimate physical examination skills: a qualitative study. *BMC Med Educ* 14, 39. doi.org/10.1186/1472-6920-14-39.

'It's hard to separate wanting to love ourselves for who we are, as we are, from the thoughts we know that certain people will have about us if we do.

Moses, G., 2020. 'Learning Not to Care What Abled Folks Think: How Internalized Ableism Affects My Body Image'. [online] *The Body Is Not an Apology*. Available at: thebodyisnotanapology.com/magazine/learning-not-to-care-what-abled-folks-think-how-internalized-ableism-affects-my-body-image/.

'It's very complex. There can be anger toward oneself and one's body for failing the person'

Darnall, B., 2020. 'Chronic Illness Can Make It Hard to Trust Your Body – Scopes'. [online] *The Paper Gown.* Available at: thepapergown.zocdoc.com/chronic-illness-can-make-it-hard-to-trust-your-body/?fbclid=IwAR2v61Dhe4ZvD-7EZiPobJ7RbDcR-Dy57wgJdCjx_BRE_qaW9NHZxF9DJSs.

Chapter 10

Our brains do their best to keep us from dwelling on our inevitable demise.

Dor-Ziderman, Y., Lutz, A. and Goldstein, A., 2019. 'Prediction-based neural mechanisms for shielding the self from existential threat'. *NeuroImage,* 202, pp.1160.

Chapter 11

It's difficult being a carer for someone with an illness'

Compassionfatigue.org, 2020. *Compassion Fatigue Awareness Project.* [online] Available at: www.compassionfatigue.org/pages/compassionfatigue.html.

This is where Ruth Pitt found herself after a successful career and a busy life as a mother of two.

Pitt, R., 2020. 'It's Hard to Be Sick When You're Single'. *The Guardian*. [online] Available at: www.theguardian.com/lifeandstyle/2013/jun/29/hard-to-be-sick-when-single.

'Having a chronic illness such as diabetes, arthritis, or multiple sclerosis can take a toll on even the best relationship.

Bruno, K., 2020. *Chronic Illness and Relationships: Communicating and Managing Stress.* [online] WebMD. Available at: www.webmd.com/sex-relationships/features/chronic-illness-seven-relationship-tips#1.

'If you're going to be afraid of something, be afraid of how a loved one's chronic condition will affect both of you,

Wilson, M., 2020. *Living in The Limbo of Chronic Illness.* [online] Thriveglobal.com. Available at: thriveglobal.com/stories/living-in-the-limbo-of-chronic-illness/.

Chapter 12

'Following a critical incident, previously held beliefs about one's self are called into question and re-evaluated.'

Ngaage, M., Agius, M., 2018, 'The Psychology of Scars: A Mini-Review', *Psychiatria Danubina*, 30 (7), pp.633–638.

'You barely slept last night, you're exhausted, and your body hurts'

Rodriguez, M., 2020. *Sick, And Sick of Pretending*. [online] Medium. Available at: medium.com/invisible-illness/sick-and-sick-of-pretending-a5cfeabc1929.

When a fistful of serious health issues struck me in my twenties, I saw how being young and female was inextricably linked to my experience.

Hirsch, M., 2018. *Invisible: How young women with serious health issues navigate work, relationships, and the pressure.* Beacon Press, Boston Massachusetts.

'Men who encounter chronic illness within their lives will engage in identity management to maintain a hegemonic masculine identity – especially when disclosing.'

Daggett, M., 2019, The Ill Man: An Exploration of Chronic Illness Disclosure within Masculine Culture, Electronic Theses and Dissertations. Paper 3567. East Tennessee State University.

'When inevitable pain arises, we take it personally.'

Brach, T., 2020. *Awakening from The Trance of Unworthiness – Tara Brach*. [online] Tara Brach. Available at: www.tarabrach.com/articles-interviews/inquiring-trance/.

'I am ashamed of being sick,'

Byczkowski, A., 2020. *In Today's Society, Chronic Illness Is Viewed as A Personal Failing.* [online] KevinMD.com. Available at: www.kevinmd.com/blog/2013/05/todays-society-chronic-illness-viewed-personal-failing.html.

'Shame becomes toxic because of premature exposure.'

Bradshaw, J., 1993. *Healing the Shame That Binds You.* Deerfield Beach: Health Communications.

Chapter 13

The experience of pregnancy with a chronic illness is one of a balancing act'

Tyer-Viola, L. & Palan Lopez, R., 2014, 'Pregnancy with Chronic Illness'. *Journal of obstetric, gynecologic, and neonatal nursing,* JOGNN/NAACOG. 43. 25-37. 10.1111/1552-6909.12275.

Chapter 14

'"You're not disabled enough."'

Abc.net.au, 2020. *Centrelink Rejected Mandy's Case for A Disability Pension Twice, Then She Fought Back.* [online] Available at: www.abc.net.au/news/2019-09-12/disability-support-pension-applicants-diverted-to-newstart/11486164.

According to a study published in Scienctific Reports in 2018, approximately 62 per cent of Australians have used complementary medicine,

Steel, A., McIntyre, E., Harnett, J., Foley, H., Adams, J., Sibbritt, D., Wardle, J., & Frawley, J., 2018. 'Complementary medicine use in the Australian population: Results of a nationally-representative cross-sectional survey'. *Scientific reports, 8* (1), 17325. doi.org/10.1038/s41598-018-35508-y.

Australian doctors have higher rates of stress and more attempts at suicide

Hoffman, R. and Bonney, A., 2018. 'Junior doctors, burnout and wellbeing: Understanding the experience of burnout in general practice registrars and hospital equivalents'. *Australian Journal of General Practice,* 47(8), pp.571–575.

Chapter 16

Life is naturally tattered, infested, bitten off, bitten into

Zuk, Marlene, 2007, *Riddled with Life; Friendly worms, ladybug sex, and the parasites that make us who we are,* Houghton Mifflin Harcourt.

www.ingramcontent.com/pod-product-compliance
Lightning Source LLC
Chambersburg PA
CBHW010719300426
44115CB00019B/2956